STRETCHING EXERCISES FOR SENIORS

A Book For Older Adults To Keep Them Pain - Free,
Flexible, And Agile. Decrease Joint Pain
And Improve Muscle Control
Effective Exercises That You Can Do At Home

NATHAN MERRICK

Table of Contents

CHAPTER 4
AFTERNOON AND EVENING STRETCHES 40

CHAPTER 5
TARGET AREA STRETCHES 58

CHAPTER 8
POST-WORKOUT STRETCHES

CHAPTER 9
TOOLS FOR STRETCHING

CHAPTER 10
POSTURE AND HOW IT AFFECTS YOUR BODY
147

CHAPTER 11
DAILY TIPS FOR STAYING FLEXIBLE 151

CHAPTER 12
HOW TO ADAPT STRETCHING WORKOUTS TO PHYSICAL LIMITATIONS 154

Introduction

Seniors are passionate about health and fitness, yet many don't know how to stick to a regular exercise routine. This book might be able to assist you! Focusing on your warm-up is the first stage in any training routine. By boosting blood flow and reducing muscular stiffness, a post-exercise warm-down activity can improve the effectiveness of a workout. Before beginning any strenuous workout, jogging for 10 minutes or jumping rope for five minutes is the best way to warm up. Seniors should avoid strenuous exercises that require twisting or turning actions and impactful routines like jogging, as these might lead to injuries later in life. Instead, strength training and aerobic exercise should be the focus of a senior's routine.

Stretching is another vital component of staying fit. Stretching improves flexibility and minimizes the chance of injury by warming up muscles before they are put to work. Stretching after an exercise is the greatest time to do it because it helps the body recover faster. Warming up before and after an exercise is crucial for staying in shape. People should always warm up before a workout by gradually walking or jogging in place to get their heart rate up, but not so quickly that they sweat excessively or breathe heavily (or they might need to stop early because of dizziness). Stretching should be done in the same way; it should be done slowly and in small, controlled motions to avoid harm.

Everyone benefits from a healthy lifestyle, but seniors benefit even more. Seniors should remember to stay hydrated at all times; the easiest method to do so is to drink enough water to avoid being dehydrated and losing energy. Any diet or training plan will be less effective when someone is thirsty. Other ways to stay healthy include eating a nutritious diet rich in fruits and vegetables, getting adequate sleep, and brushing your teeth twice a day.

Families should pay special attention to their parents' health, as aging might make it more difficult for them to maintain their health. Seniors' fitness routines may not be enough; they may need to raise the intensity of their workouts. Seniors should also avoid strenuous activities that require twisting or turning motions because these might cause injuries later in life. Instead, strength training and aerobic exercise should be the focus of a senior's routine.

Another essential component of staying healthy is stretching. Stretching improves flexibility and minimizes the chance of injury by warming up muscles before they are put to work. Stretching should be done after an exercise because it aids in the body's recovery. People should always warm up before a workout by gradually walking or running in place to raise their heart rate.

Stretching should be done in the same way; it should be done slowly and in small, controlled motions to avoid harm.

Benefits of Stretching

Stretching exercises to strengthen your muscles are essential since the age-related loss of muscle mass and strength, joined with reduced activity levels, can lead to many issues. In fact, research suggests that inactive adults over 65 have weaker balance and are more likely to be disabled by falls than those who live an active lifestyle.

The following are some of the medical benefits of stretching exercises for seniors to assist you in better understanding the benefits of this sort of exercise:

- Stretching improves your body's fluid movement. As a result, increased circulation oxygenates cells and tissues, potentially lowering heart disease risk factors such as high blood pressure.
- Stretching extends the range of motion in the body. Stretching your muscles allows your joints and bones to move more easily, which improves balance and mobility. Regular stretching exercises can also make you feel healthier because they give you a general sense of well-being.
- As you get older, stretching helps to relieve joint tightness, aches, and pains. If performing a movement causes pain or discomfort, the body likely has

to be stretched more to loosen up the tissue surrounding the joint so that activities at that joint can be performed without pain. In addition, stretching improves circulation, which nourishes tissues and removes poisons from them throughout the body.

- Stretching exercises are a great technique to warm up your muscles before a strength training session. Warm muscles are suppler and can stretch further when opposed to cold muscles.
- Stretching should be done every day if you want to keep your muscle strength and flexibility. It should be a part of your daily practice to help prevent injuries from worsening and to help you recover from injuries more quickly when they do occur.

Chapter 1

Stretching

The Types of Stretching

When we think of stretching, we may remember how we used to stretch when we were in an elementary school physical education class. Do you remember standing and bending over, trying to touch your feet while bouncing from the waist? Or sitting on the floor, legs apart, and trying to touch your toes while stretching and bouncing? This type of stretching is known as ballistic stretching. The premise of ballistic stretching is to use force, gravity, or momentum to stretch your muscle past its normal range of motion by repeatedly bouncing or pushing. While this stretching mode has fallen out of favor because of the increased possibility of muscle tears and pulls, some professional athletes and dancers still use it. However, this type of stretching is not recommended for most people, and especially not for older adults.

Popular in today's medical and fitness worlds are dynamic stretching and static stretching. What is the difference between the two? Dynamic stretching is used before exercise, team sports, or any strenuous activity.

The purpose of dynamic stretching is to get the muscles ready that you will be using in the activity by increasing the temperature of the muscles and decreasing any muscle stiffness. These stretches slowly take your muscles and joints through the range of motion before you perform them with more intensity and speed. Examples of dynamic stretches are walking lunges, torso twists, arm circles, and leg swings. Many dynamic stretches are sport-specific, meaning they mimic the movement you will be doing in your particular sport or workout.

Static stretching is used after exercise to help you cool down and stretch out muscles, but it is also used as part of a routine stretching program to help maintain flexibility and mobility in your muscles and joints. Stretching a muscle as far as it can go without pain and holding the stretch for 30 to 60 seconds is the basic idea of static stretching. Holding a stretched position helps lengthen your muscles, increasing flexibility, and helps relax your muscles. Examples of static stretches are hamstring stretch, side bends, and hip flexor stretch. Static stretches are done standing, sitting, or lying down.

When to Stretch

We have already touched on the importance of stretching before exercising or activity and afterward. The pre-activity stretches are meant to warm up muscles for an increase in muscular activity through exercise, dance, or other sports. These stretches don't help with flexibility, but are preparation for increased movement. Post-activity stretches are done while you are cooling down from an exercise or activity. Your muscles are easier to stretch because they are warm and supple, making them more flexible. But what about other times of the day that stretching can be done?

Stretching in the morning just after waking up is a great way to release tension and to help you gently wake up your body. The body heals and does repair work on itself while you are sleeping, including repair of muscles and other soft tissue (Walker, 2010). When you awaken in the morning, increasing your circulation brings blood and oxygen into your muscles at a higher rate and gets your body ready for the day's events ahead. Morning stretches also help wake up your joints and alleviate any stiffness from them being still and immobile most of the night.

A short stretch break done several times during the day is helpful to keep joints and muscles loose and moving. If you do a lot of sitting for work or in your leisure time, it's essential to get up and stretch your neck, upper back, lower back, and hips to keep them limber. Stretch breaks are also great ways to take a mental break from whatever work or activity you are doing. By concentrating on your body and the movements it is making as you stretch, along with some focused breathing, you can return to your work relaxed and renewed.

Most people do not think of stretching in the evening before going to bed, but this is a great time to stretch! Your muscles and soft tissues like ligaments and tendons are repaired while you sleep. By stretching in the evening, you elongate and lengthen your muscles. This increased muscle length allows the repair and healing work to be done along with the entire muscle (Walker, 2010). Also, stretching before bedtime is a way to wind down and relax. The slow, rhythmic movements of a gentle stretching routine and measured breathing help signal the body and mind that sleep is coming.

Where to Stretch

The best place to stretch is anywhere you have enough space and are comfortable. It could be in your bedroom, living room, home gym, backyard, or garage. It is also possible to stretch outdoors at a park, beach, or open-air sports facility. The important thing is to check the surroundings to make sure you stretch on a surface level to avoid imbalances or falls. Having a padded exercise or yoga mat can be helpful, especially if you are doing stretches that involve kneeling, sitting, or lying on the ground. Seated stretches can be done from a chair at your desk, dining room table, or even in your car.

How to Stretch

Stretching requires more than just bending over and reaching for your toes. Proper form such as breathing, variety, and alignment contributes to getting the most out of your stretching routine. Being aware of common mistakes and avoiding them is also essential.

Breathing seems like a natural thing to do. We all do it several thousand times a day. Proper breathing allows for the full expansion of your entire lungs. Many people breathe by taking shallow breaths that cause their chest to rise and fall and their waist to contract and get small. These types of breaths miss filling the lower part of your lungs. The proper way to breathe, sometimes called belly breathing, is to breathe into your belly and diaphragm area. To do this, sit or lie down comfortably and breathe in through your nose. Your chest and belly should expand and then exhale through your mouth. Belly breathing takes some practice but gets easier as you practice it more.

Doing some stretching every day is a good idea, especially if you are working on flexibility or recovery of a particular muscle. However, just as you wouldn't eat the same thing every day or do the same exercise day in and day out, you also don't want to do the same stretches all the time. So it's important to include several different types of stretches to avoid any muscle imbalance or overworking of muscles.

Good posture and body alignment are essential to avoid strain and injury, and this also applies to stretching. Maintaining proper posture and good form as you stretch helps ensure that the muscles you are targeting are being stretched correctly and that you are not putting unnecessary pressure on your neck or other joints. There is a tendency for some people to scrunch their shoulders or hunch over while stretching. This causes imbalance and undue tension in those areas that may lead to injury. Maintain good posture and alignment by keeping your back straight (but not rigid), shoulders down and away from your ears, and a relaxed jaw.

According to the Stretch Coach, author and stretching guru Brad Walker, people make some common mistakes when they begin to stretch (Walker, 2010).

These include:

- Holding your breath. This causes muscles to tense up and become difficult to stretch. Instead, breathe deeply, utilizing the belly breathing technique to relax muscles and increase circulation.
- Forgetting to warm up. Walker likens this to stretching old, dry rubber bands. They don't stretch very far and may snap. Instead, use five minutes to warm up your muscles by walking in place to increase muscle temperature and make them more pliable.
- Stretching an injury. Avoid any stretching done at least for the first 72 hours if injured. Very gentle and light static stretching can be done for the first two weeks. After that, some dynamic stretching can slowly be reintroduced into your stretching routine.
- Stretching to the point of pain. Our muscles react with a built-in safety reflex when we stretch too hard. As a consequence, they naturally contract to get away

and protect the body from the pain. So stretch only to where it is comfortable and with slight tension.

- Not holding the stretch long enough. Holding the position for just a few seconds may feel like a stretch, but it isn't long enough for the muscle to relax and lengthen. It is important to hold a stretch position for 30 to 60 seconds, take about two or three deep breaths, and repeat the stretch twice or more.

Stretching is beneficial to our bodies and especially so as we grow older. However, it is not a quick fix. It will take time to see the results of a regular stretching routine, but the benefits to your body and well-being are worth it!

Chapter 2

Stretching for Pain Prevention

Stretching Without Pain

Stretching should only provide a slight sensation of 'tightness' or tension in the pulled muscle. When stretching, pain signals an injury or an overstretched muscle. Stop stretching immediately if you feel any pain, and never stretch beyond a 'pleasant tightness.'

Stretches Should Be Repeated After Resting

A single stretching for each target muscle is good; however, two stretches for every muscle, followed by a 30-second pause, will help you extend the range of motion even further.

Stretching Should Be Done Twice a Week

Stretch the major muscles after each workout if possible, but stretching twice a week is a good compromise if it is too time demanding.

Rather than detracting from your other workouts, swapping some stretching for a few more minutes of aerobic or resistance training will improve, not diminish, your total fitness. If you can stretch for two ten-minute sessions per week, you'll be well on your way to being mobile, supple, and injury-free.

Do's and Don'ts of Stretching

Simply follow the dos and don'ts given below to ensure that you stretch safely and get the most out of your stretching.

'Dos' of Stretching

- Make sure the muscles you're stretching are appropriately warmed up.
- After your workout, stretch and relax
- Breathe freely.
- Each stretch should be held for at least 30 seconds.
- Stretching should be done all throughout the body to avoid postural abnormalities.
- Use the proper technique.
- Maintain a stretch for a few seconds.
- Take a deep breath.

Don'ts of Stretching

- Stretching must never be painful, so avoid it.
- Don'ts' be pushed to their limits.
- Stretching cold muscles is a surefire way to injure yourself.
- If you bounce or rock while holding a stretch, you may overstretch and injure yourself.

Time spent restoring the length of shortened, tight muscles will bring far greater and longer-term advantages than a few extra minutes at the gym or a few extra miles on the road. You won't lose it if you follow these stretching do's and don'ts given above regularly.

Chapter 3

Morning Stretches

A morning stretch after a night's rest is an excellent way to wake up, but it is also a way to relax muscles that have been stagnant and still all night. Our heart rate slows down, muscles relax, and blood flow slows down when we sleep. It is a time when our body can rest and rejuvenate. That is why it is common when waking up for our body to be stiff because of muscle inactivity while resting. This is especially true if you sleep in the same position all night. Also, while we sleep, the fluid increases in our joints and spine, leading to extra stiffness and morning aches (Stretch22, n.d.)

As we get older, this stiffness can be somewhat painful when combined with arthritis or other health challenges and can linger throughout the morning. Stretching helps alleviate this stiffness and joint discomfort. It also gets the body moving and ready for the day ahead. In addition, by stretching in the morning regularly, you are increasing the mobility of your muscles and joints. The increased mobility and flexibility can prevent future injury.

Remember that morning stretches are your body's chance to awaken, increase the blood flow, and get the muscles warmed up. Because muscles can be very tight in the morning, your range of flexibility is less than it would be later in the day. You will not be able to stretch as far or as deep as you normally would, but that is perfectly okay. Be especially careful not to do any bouncing or bobbing while doing the stretches, as this can cause pulled or torn muscles. It is important to be kind to your body, especially so early in the day. Stretching in the morning should feel good!

Most of the upper body stretches can be done standing or sitting, so choose what is most appropriate for you. Doing the stretches while standing helps energize your body in the morning, but if you can't stand for any time, it is fine to sit while performing the stretches. The lower body stretches are done on the floor, but use a padded mat if it is more comfortable for you. A padded mat is essential if you have any knee pain or hip issues. Since these are stretches that are done in the morning, you can do these stretches in your bedroom if you have the space. Almost all of the stretches, except for a few lower body stretches, can even be done in your pajamas while still in bed! Use common sense and precautions to be sure your bed and surroundings are safe to perform any stretching exercises before starting.

You do not have to do all the stretches in this chapter every morning unless you want to. However, if pressed for time, choose one upper body and one lower body stretch and do just those. Even stretching for five minutes is a helpful start to your day.

Overhead Stretch

Areas stretched: chest, shoulders, triceps, lats, and front of the neck.

Instructions:

1. Standing with feet about hip-width apart, raise both arms above your head.
2. Interlace your fingers, and raise your hands and arms upward as if trying to touch the ceiling. Breathe in deeply and then exhale.
3. If comfortable, look up and point your chin straight in front of you. Deep breath and exhale. If you have any neck pain or neck issues, skip this step.

4. With hands still raised, slightly bend the upper body backward and hold for 2 or 3 seconds, then return to standing straight.
5. Lower arms back down to sides.
6. Repeat the stretch two or three times.

Take note:

- This can be done seated if you are unsteady on your feet or if you have any vertigo or balance issues.

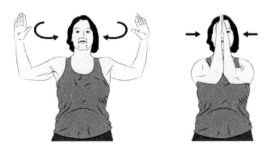

Cactus Arms

Areas stretched: front of the shoulder, chest.

Instructions:

1. From a standing or seated position, raise arms overhead and then lower to bend at the elbow to form 90° angles, palms facing forward. Your arms should form a cactus or football goal post shape.
2. With arms still raised and bent, push your chest forward as you push your arms slightly backward. Take a deep breath, then exhale and bring your chest and arms back to normal.
3. Repeat two or three times.

Take note:

- Protect your lower back if you are standing or sitting by not arching your lower back while doing this stretch. If you find you are arching, you can do this stretch lying on your back and taking care to keep your lower back pressed to the floor.

Neck Roll Stretch

Areas stretched: back and sides of neck, trapezius.

Instructions:

1. From a standing or seated position, look straight ahead. Slowly tilt your head to the left as if your left ear was trying to touch the top of your left shoulder. Be sure your shoulders do not hunch up! Instead, keep them relaxed and down. Take a deep breath in and then exhale.
2. Slowly roll your head down so that your chin is pointing towards your chest. Remember to keep the shoulders relaxed. Deep breath in and then exhale.
3. Roll your head to the right. Your right ear should be

facing down as if to touch the top of your right shoulder. Deep breath in and then exhale. Slowly bring the head back to a neutral, upright position. You can use your hands to help your head come back to upright gently.

4. Repeat two or three times. You can alternate sides by starting with the right side first.

Take note:

- Never tilt your head back while doing neck rolls. This puts a lot of unnecessary compression on your neck and spine.

Seated Spinal Twist

Areas stretched: entire back, upper gluteus.

Instructions:

1. Sitting on the floor cross-legged, sit up tall and gently twist your upper body to the right. Place your left hand on your right knee and your right hand on the floor behind you.
2. If you can, look to the back over your right shoulder. If not, keep your head relaxed and look ahead or down. Take a deep breath in, then exhale.

3. Return your upper body and head back to the front. Take a deep breath in, then exhale.

4. Change the cross of your legs, now put the other leg in front.

5. Sit up tall and gently twist your upper body to the left. Place your right hand on your left knee and your left hand on the floor behind you.

6. Look to the back over your left shoulder, if possible. Otherwise, relax your neck and look ahead or down. Take a deep breath in, and then exhale.

7. Return your upper body and head back to the front. Repeat the stretch two or three more times.

Take note:

- Keep both glutes firmly on the ground. If one side is lifting up, you are twisting too far. Only twist as far as you are comfortable.

Cat and Cow

Areas stretched: upper back, mid-back, back of the neck, shoulders.

Instructions:

1. Get on your hands and knees on the floor. Your hands should be directly under your shoulders and your knees directly under your hips. Your back should be neutral and roughly parallel to the floor.
2. Take a deep breath and inhale while gently lifting your head and your tailbone. Your back will arch slightly, and your belly will hang and be loose. This is called the cow stretch.
3. While exhaling, gently lower your chin towards your chest as you round your upper back towards the ceiling. Keep your tailbone, and your abdominals tucked in but don't clench them. This portion is called the cat stretch.
4. Repeat the cow and cat stretches slowly, flowing from one to the other, several times.

Take note:

- Keep your shoulders away from your ears and relax while doing this stretch. There should not be any tension in your neck or shoulders.

- If your wrists cannot support you, a variation of this stretch can be done seated. Sit cross-legged and place your hands on your knees while doing the cat and cow stretches.

Seated Forward Bend

Areas stretched: Entire back of the body, including calves, hamstrings, and back.

Instructions:

1. Sit on the floor with your legs together and stretched forward. Legs can be slightly apart.
2. Raise both arms overhead with palms facing each other. Take a deep breath in and then exhale.
3. While exhaling, bend your upper body forward from the hip joint. Keep your neck in a neutral position and your back straight. It is okay to have a slight bend at your knees; they don't have to be perfectly straight
4. Bring your arms down and let your hands rest on the floor with palms facing up.
5. Repeat the stretch by raising arms overhead and starting again. Do this two or three more times.

Take note:

- Remember not to bounce when folding forward and don't force yourself to try to go lower. Hamstrings and calves are naturally tight in the morning. This should be a reasonably passive stretch that just loosens up the back of the legs and back.

Foot Point and Flex

Areas stretched: toes, feet, ankles, calves.

Instructions:

1. In a seated position on the floor with your legs stretched forward, point your feet and toes. Stretch them as far away from you as you can. Take a deep breath in and then exhale.
2. In the same seated position, flex your feet and toes back so that toes point up to the ceiling and maybe even flex towards you. Take a deep breath in and then exhale.
3. Repeat the stretch two or three more times.

Take note:

- This stretch can be done seated in a chair if the floor is too uncomfortable. You can also stretch one foot at a time if you find it too hard to do both feet at the same time.

Half-Kneeling Hip Flexor Stretch

Areas stretched: hip flexor, quads.

Instructions:

1. Start on the floor by coming down on all fours with both hands and both knees on the ground. Get into a half-kneeling position by lifting the left knee and bringing the left foot forward in front of you. The left foot should be directly under the left knee.
2. Raise so that your body is upright and your right knee is on the ground directly below your right hip. Both knees should be at a 90° angle and hands on your hips. Take a deep breath in and exhale.
3. While exhaling, move hips forward. Your weight will transfer to your left foot, and you will feel the front of your right hip stretch. Keep an upright posture. Take a deep breath in and then exhale. Move hips back to starting position.

4. Repeat the stretch two or three more times on the same leg. Then, switch legs to stretch your other hip flexor.

Take note:

- Hip flexors are tight in most people, and that contributes to back pain. Take this stretch slowly and allow your hip flexor to relax. As you do this stretch more regularly, you will be able to come forward farther.
- If you are stable and confident in this stretch, you can make it more challenging by lifting your arms above your head while stretching.

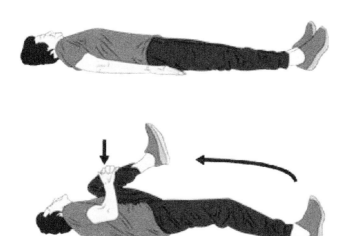

Lying Knees to Chest

Areas stretched: lower back, hips, glutes, hamstrings.

Instructions:

1. Lie down on your back, resting your legs and arms on the floor.
2. Bring your left knee up towards your chest and place your hands either on top or behind your knee to support your leg. Don't tug or pull on your leg. Instead, take a deep breath in and then exhale. Return your leg to the starting position.
3. Draw your right knee up towards your chest and either place your hands on top of the knee or behind it. Remember not to pull on your leg. Instead, take a deep breath in and then exhale. Return your leg back down to the floor.
4. Repeat the sequence two or three more times.

Take note:

- Once you are comfortable and confident in this stretch, you can make it more challenging by drawing up both knees simultaneously. Either place hands on top of knees or one hand behind each knee for support.

All Fours Side Bend

Areas stretched: sides of hips, torso, and neck.

Instructions:

1. Get on all fours on the floor with hands directly below shoulders and knees directly below hips.
2. Pick up the left leg and bring it over the right leg and foot. Then, place the left foot on the floor as far to the right as you can comfortably get it.
3. Look over the right shoulder and back at your foot. Take a deep breath, lean into your left hip, and then exhale. You should feel the stretch along the entire left side of your body.
4. Bring the left leg back to the starting position. Breathe in and out.

5. Now, pick up the right leg and take it over the other leg and foot. Place the right foot on the floor as far to the left as possible.

6. Look over the left shoulder and back at your foot. Take a deep breath, lean into your right hip this time, and then exhale. Feel the stretch along the right side of your body. Bring legs back to the starting position.

7. Repeat the stretch on both legs two more times.

Take note:

• This is a deep stretch along the sides of the body and should feel good, especially in the morning. If you have neck issues, you don't have to look over your shoulder if it causes any pain. You can just concentrate on stretching the lower body.

Chapter 4

Afternoon and Evening Stretches

S tretching in the evening and just before bedtime is a wonderful way to wind down. Unfortunately, many people have a difficult time falling asleep at night. Sometimes the inability to relax before bedtime is related to our muscles feeling restless. If you have had a day of sitting in a chair at work, sitting in a car, or just sitting at home, your muscles need some movement and stretching to release the tension that has built up during the day. Along with releasing the tension, stretching also increases circulation and blood flow to tense muscles (Sleep Advisor, 2020). Once the muscles have been stretched and relaxed, you will be less likely to toss and turn once you get into bed to go to sleep. This increase in the quality of your sleep is a benefit to you and your partner, who may awaken when you sleep restlessly.

When you relax the body, it's natural for your mind also to relax and get ready for sleep. By doing a regular nighttime stretching routine, your mind and body know it is the time that they can enter into a calming, loosening, and relaxing state. This focused state of deliberately relaxing helps you separate the activity phase of your day from the restful phase of your night.

Slow and deliberate breathing while performing these stretches also contributes to entering into a relaxed state. If you find that you are inadvertently holding your breath while stretching, you may be stretching too intensely or too fast. Your goal is to deepen and slow your breathing. Relaxing your body and mind allows you to release the stress and tension of the day and leave it behind. This release may help you fall asleep faster and stay asleep longer.

If desired, you can take a warm bath or shower before performing these stretching exercises. This helps wash off your day both mentally and physically. It also adds a marker to your evening routine that signals that sleep is coming to both body and mind. Performing the evening stretches after a warm shower also warms up the muscles before stretching.

Most of the evening stretches are done low to the ground and can even be done in bed if you choose. If the stretches are done on the floor, do them on a padded mat or on your bedroom carpet. As always, look at your bed and surroundings to ensure they are safe to perform these stretching exercises on and use common sense.

Remember, you do not have to do every stretch in this chapter every evening. The goal is to unwind and loosen up, so choose one upper body stretch and one lower body stretch to do in the evening. Taking just five minutes to stretch before bedtime will help you relax before drifting off to sleep.

Bear Hug

Areas stretched: upper and middle back, including trapezius and shoulder blades.

Instructions:

1. From a standing or seated position, raise both arms out from the sides of your body, palms facing forward. Take a deep breath in and then exhale.
2. Take another deep breath in and gently cross your arms in front of you, right arm over left. Exhaling, hug yourself. Your hands should be touching the back of your shoulders. Hold this position and breathe in and out slowly two more times.
3. Release your arms and bring them back to your sides.
4. Breathing deep, gently cross your arms again with your left arm over your right. Exhale and hug yourself. You may be able to bring your hands onto your shoulder blades, but if not, just keep them on your

shoulders. Hold this position and slowly breathe in and out two more times.

5. Release your arms. Repeat if you desire or move on to another stretch.

Take note:

- Depending on the length of your arms and the size of your chest, you may or may not be able to touch your shoulder blades. The goal here is to stretch the muscles of your upper back.
- Remember not to scrunch up your shoulders. Keep them down and away from your ears.

Seated Overhead Side Stretch

Areas stretched: entire sides of the body, neck, upper arms.

Instructions:

1. From a seated position, sitting cross-legged, raise your left arm above your head and reach for the ceiling. Take a deep breath in.
2. Bend your head and torso to the right while looking straight ahead as you exhale. If it is okay for you, let your neck relax and allow your head to also bend to the right. You can place the other hand on the floor for balance. Take a slow, deep breath in and then exhale. Breathe in and out a couple of more times before returning to the starting position.
3. Change the cross of your legs. Raise your right arm and reach for the ceiling. Take a deep breath in.
4. Exhaling, bend your head and torso to the left while keeping your gaze straight ahead. If possible, let your neck relax and let your head also bend to the left.

Place your other hand on the floor for balance if you need to. Slowly breathe in and then exhale. Breathe in and out a few more times and then return to the starting position.

Take note:

- Don't allow your chest to fall forward or your shoulders to round during this stretch. Instead, maintain good posture while doing this stretch by engaging your abdominal core muscles.
- Be sure to keep both glutes firmly on the floor. If one or the other is lifting up as you stretch to the side, you are stretching too far.

Thread the Needle

Areas stretched: shoulders, upper arms, neck, spine.

Instructions:

1. Get on the floor on all fours. Hands should be directly under your shoulders and knees directly under your hips.
2. Take your left hand and thread it under your right arm and just above the floor. Continue extending your left arm along the floor as you bring your left

shoulder to the floor. Let your left-hand rest on the floor, palm facing up. Your left ear should be resting on the floor as well.

3. Slide the other hand along the floor until it is above your head, palm down, so it is touching the floor just past your head. If this is too much, just leave your right hand where it is. Take a deep, slow breath in and then exhale. Your neck should be relaxed. Breathe slowly in and out two more times. Slowly lift your shoulder up and return to starting position.

4. Take your right hand and thread it under your left arm to do the other side. Extend your right arm along the floor and let it rest your hand on the floor, palm facing up. Bring your right shoulder down and rest it on the floor, along with your right ear.

5. Slide the other hand on the floor until it is above your head, palm facing down. Again, if this is too much, you can leave your left hand where it is. Take a deep breath in and then exhale. Be sure your neck is re-laxed, and breathe slowly in and out two more times. Slowly lift your shoulder up and return to starting po-sition.

Take note:

•   If this stretch is too much pressure on your wrists, you can start this on your knees and forearms on the ground. Then, continue the stretch by keeping your weight on your forearm as you slide the other hand and arm underneath the armpit.

- Depending on your lower back strength, you may need to avoid bringing your shoulder down all the way to the floor. If this is the case, you can place a pillow or cushion under your shoulder for it to rest on as you thread the needle.

Floor Angels

Areas stretched: chest, triceps, lats.

Instructions:

1. Lie on the floor facing up with legs straight and arms down by your side. Inhale deeply and slowly, and then exhale.
2. Inhale while sliding your arms along the floor until they are above your head, palms up, as if you were making "snow angels" in the snow! Stretch your arms

and lengthen your body as much as you are able.

3. Exhale as you bring your arm back down to your sides.

4. Repeat the stretch two or three more times.

Take note:

- Once you are comfortable doing this stretch, you can add your legs by sliding your legs apart as you slide your arms up.

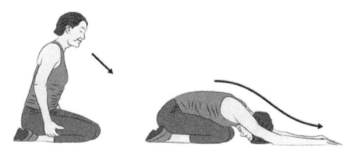

Child's Pose

Areas stretched: shoulders, back of the neck.

Instructions:

1. Get on the floor on your hands and knees. Your hands should be directly under your shoulders, and your knees should be directly under your hips. Take a deep breath in.

2. Lean back as you exhale and bring your glutes down and back to your feet. Lower your torso towards the floor and extend your arms along the floor up over your head. You should be facing the floor, and your

forehead may be able to come down to the ground. Stretch your arms as much as you can while breathing in deep. Slowly exhale. Take two or three more breaths in this position before returning to the starting position.

Take note:

- If your glutes cannot touch your heels, you can place a pillow or rolled up towel between your hamstrings and calves for support.
- Be sure not to scrunch up your shoulders when doing this stretch. The neck should be long and shoulders away from the ears.

Banana Stretch

Areas stretched: sides of body including obliques, lats, hips.

Instructions:

1. Lie on the floor, face up towards the ceiling. Stretch your arms up overhead with your hands resting on the floor above you. Stretch your legs out straight. Take a deep, slow breath in.
2. Slide your arms and legs along the floor to the left as you exhale. If you can't do both simultaneously, you can slide your arms first and then your legs. You should be in a banana shape and feel a stretch along the right side of your body.
3. Hold this banana shape and breathe in and out slowly two or three times. Return to the starting position.
4. Slide your arms and legs along the floor to the right to stretch your other side. Now you should feel the stretch on your left side. Hold the shape and breath in and out slowly two or three times. Return to the starting position.

Take note:

- You can deepen this stretch if you desire. For example, as your arms and legs are sliding to the left, let your left hand grab your right wrist and gently pull. This increases the stretch in your lats and rib cage. If you are sliding to the right, your right hand will grab your left wrist.
- To deepen the stretch in your hips and IT band, cross your right ankle over your left ankle as your legs slide to the left. Cross your left ankle over your right one if your legs are sliding to the right.

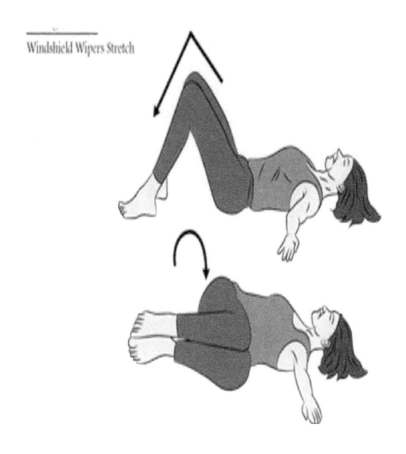

Windshield Wipers Stretch

Windshield Wipers Stretch

Areas stretched: internal and external hip muscles, tops of quads.

Instructions:

1. Lie on the floor on your back, facing up. Bend your knees so they are pointing up to the ceiling and your feet are flat on the floor, hip-width distance apart. Bring your arms out into a T-position.
2. Take a deep breath in. Slowly let both knees fall to

the left as you exhale. Inhale as you bring your knees back up. Slowly let both knees now fall to the right and exhale.

3. Repeat the windshield wiper motion, left and right, slowly two or three more times.

Take note:

- Only let your legs fall to the side as far as it is comfortable for your hips. Keep your arms out in a T-position to help stabilize your torso as your legs go back and forth.

- A variation of this stretch can be done seated. Lean back and support your body with your hands behind you as your legs fall back and forth.

Reclined Figure Four

Areas stretched: glutes, hamstrings, hips, lower back.

Instructions:

1. Lie on the floor, facing up. Bend your knees so they are pointing up to the ceiling and your feet are flat on the floor.
2. Bring your right leg up and cross your leg to form a figure four. Your right ankle should be resting on your left leg near your knee. Take a deep breath in and then exhale.
3. Let your hands grab behind your left thigh and bring your left leg towards your chest slowly and gently. Keep both feet flexed to protect your knees. Take a deep inhale and then exhale as you bring your feet back to the ground and uncross your legs.
4. To stretch the other side, bring your left leg up so that your left ankle rests on your right leg. If you can, grab behind your right leg this time and bring it towards you.
5. Inhale slowly and exhale. Uncross your legs and bring both feet back to the ground.

Take note:

• Depending on the mobility of your hips, just bringing your ankle up and placing it on top of your other leg may be enough of a stretch for you. Don't feel you have to draw the other leg towards you if you aren't able to.

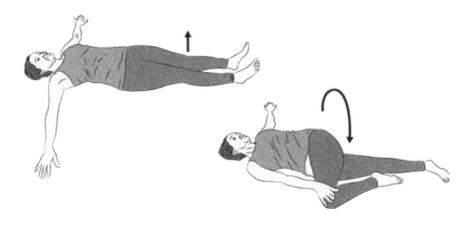

Lying Spinal Twist

Areas stretched: glutes, obliques, chest.

Instructions:

1. Lie on your back on the floor, facing up. Bend your knees so that they are pointing up towards the ceiling and keep your feet next to each other. Bring your arms out into a T-position.
2. Taking a deep breath in. As you exhale, allow both knees to fall to the right until they reach the ground.

Your hips should be stacked one on top of the other. If you can, turn your head and look to the left to get a neck stretch.

3. Inhale and then exhale as you bring your knees back up.
4. To stretch the other side, breath in and exhale as both knees now fall to the left until they touch the floor.
5. Again, hips are stacked on top of each other. Look to the right if you can. Take a deep breath and exhale before returning to the starting position.

Take note:

- Don't force your knees to the floor. If you cannot twist that far, place a pillow or cushion to the side and let your knees rest on that.
- Both shoulders should remain flat on the floor, and your chest should be facing the ceiling the whole time. If your shoulder is lifting up, you are twisting too far.

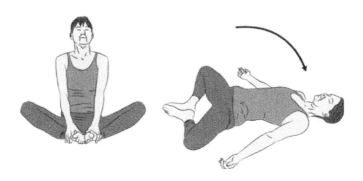

Reclined Butterfly

Areas stretched: hips, inner thighs, groin muscles.

Instructions:

1. Lie on your back on the floor with your legs straight and your hands by your sides.
2. Take a deep breath in and slowly exhale as you bend the knees and bring the soles of your feet together. Your legs and feet should roughly form a diamond shape. Your knees may or may not touch the floor, depending on the mobility of your hips. Hold this position and breathe in and out slowly two or three times. Then, return to the starting position.

Take note:

- Depending on your flexibility, your feet may be close or far from your groin. Move your feet to where it is most comfortable for you and your inner thigh muscles. For added stretch, you can slide your arms along the floor up above your head.

Chapter 5

Target Area Stretches

Back

Lower-back pain is one of the leading causes of work-related disabilities. Not only are the muscles of the back where we often carry stress, but they are also prone to injuries from lifting and twisting movements. Back stretches greatly improve the flexibility and resilience of your entire spine, from your neck to your tailbone.

Child's Pose

AFFECTED AREAS

- Lower back: quadratus lumborum, erector spinae
- Middle back: latissimus dorsi, lower trapezius, serratus anterior.

GOOD FOR

- Child's pose is an excellent stretch to loosen your entire spine, from your lower back all the way to your shoulders. Proper breathing during this stretch will also get your blood flowing.

LEVEL UP

- Reach with your right arm under your chest so it's perpendicular to your left arm. Turn your torso slightly to your left to feel the deep stretch in your right shoulder. Hold for 30 seconds and repeat on the opposite side.

ON THE FLY

- Deep inhalations and exhalations intensify this stretch and increase your lung capacity and enhance oxygen circulation through your body.

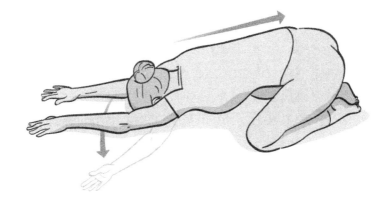

Instructions:

1. Begin by kneeling on all four with your hands in the line below your shoulders and your hips in line with your knees.
2. Inhale deeply to prepare, and slowly exhale while lowering your hips down to your heels.
3. Extend your arms straight ahead of you, sliding your hands forward.
4. Rest your forehead on the floor, and breathe deeply for 30 seconds.
5. Slowly rise to the neutral position, and perform three repetitions.

Cat-Cow Stretch

AFFECTED AREAS

- Lower back: quadratus lumborum, erector spinae
- Middle back: latissimus dorsi, lower trapezius, serratus anterior
- Abdomen: transverse abdominus

GOOD FOR

- A safe and simple beginner stretch, the Cat-Cow, is a full-body warm-up exercise. If you're looking for a great stretch to start your morning, this yoga stretch is for you. It's also a fantastic way to release tension in your shoulders and find relief for lower back pain.

LEVEL UP

Work on your balancing skills with this yoga variation called Tiger Pose. From the kneeling position on all fours, extend your right leg behind as you lift your head and chest upward. Next, curl your back as you bend your knee and bring your head downward. Finally, gently touch your knee to your forehead. Repeat ten times per side.

REMEMBER

Move slowly through this stretch. As you curl your back, think of progressing one vertebra at a time, keeping your shoulders back and away from your ears.

Instructions:

1. Begin by kneeling on all four with your hands in the line below your shoulders and your hips in line with your knees. Lengthen your neck and roll your shoulders back.
2. Inhale and scoop your abdomen toward the floor, arching your back, and gaze forward.
3. As you exhale, tuck in your abdomen and slowly curl your back toward the ceiling while tucking in your chin toward your chest. Think of forming an upside-down U with your body.
4. Hold for a moment and inhale as you return to the neutral position.
5. Repeat 10 to 15 times.

Door-Assisted Side Bend

AFFECTED AREAS

- Back: latissimus dorsi, teres major, teres minor, erector spinae
- Abdomen: abdominal obliques

GOOD FOR

- Many of us favor one side of our body and build tightness around overused muscles. This deep side bend lengthens the muscles in the middle of your back, one side at a time, so you can target the areas that need more flexibility.

LEVEL UP

- Intensify the stretch by placing your hands higher on the doorframe. You'll engage more muscles all through the side of your body and along your spine.

ON THE FLY

- This side bend is a very effective, deep stretch that you can perform anywhere you find a door.

Instructions:

1. Stand straight with your feet together and about an arm's distance to the left of a doorframe.
2. Keeping your body facing forward, grab the edge of the doorframe with both hands, left over right, at about shoulder height.
3. Lean away from the doorframe, shifting your hips toward your left.
4. Hold for 30 seconds and repeat three times per side.

Wall-Assisted Upper-Back Stretch

AFFECTED AREAS

- Upper back: latissimus dorsi, trapezius
- Neck: levator scapula, spelenius capitus

GOOD FOR

- Poor posture and slouching can often lead to upper back pain, as can prolonged hours sitting at a desk or driving a car. This simple stretch targets your upper and middle back muscles, lengthening the muscles along your spine and releasing pressure between your shoulder blades.

LEVEL UP

- Engage additional muscles along the sides of your neck by turning your head slowly to your right and holding for five seconds. Then, repeat to the opposite side.

REMEMBER

- Imagine someone is trying to pull you away from the wall. Keep your back straight and try to lengthen through your arms and your spine as you lower your head and shoulders.

Instructions:

1. Stand facing a wall with your feet hip-width apart.
2. Press your palms into the wall at shoulder height.
3. Step about two feet away from the wall.
4. Turn your gaze down at your feet and pull your shoulders away from the wall while pressing your hands firmly into the wall.
5. Hold for 30 seconds and repeat three to four times.

Shoulders and Chest

Shoulders are often the repository of accumulated daily stress, tightening and rising toward the ears. The chest, meanwhile, often becomes cramped and concave after spending hours working at a desk. The following stretches can help open both areas and restore proper posture.

Posterior Arm Cradle

AFFECTED AREAS

Front of shoulders: anterior deltoids

Chest: pectorals

GOOD FOR

- This peaceful, seated stretch eases strain in the front of your shoulders while opening your chest and lengthening your neck. If you're feeling stressed or simply longing to open the front of your body, this is the stretch for you.

LEVEL UP

- Hold the stretch for a deeper opening through your chest and lengthening along your spine, and slowly tilt your head forward, bringing your chin into your chest. Slowly tilt your head backward, raising your forehead to the ceiling.

ON THE FLY

- This stretch can be done at home, in the office, or while standing, which makes it a great on-the-move option.

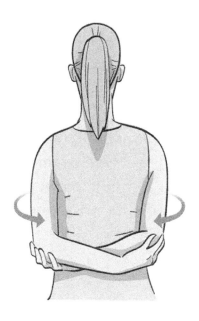

Instructions:

1. Find a comfortable place to sit, either on the floor or in a chair. Place your palms on your thighs and inhale.
2. Exhale as you push your shoulders down and roll them slightly back while lengthening your neck.
3. Gently bend your right arm behind your back and let it rest behind your hip. Bring your left hand behind your back to meet your right hand.
4. Slowly walk your hands in toward each other and up your forearms, settling at the opposite elbow.
5. Open your chest wide and breathe deeply and slowly for 30 to 45 seconds.

Arm Stretch Lying Down

AFFECTED AREAS

- Full body

GOOD FOR

- Try this exercise if your core muscles are a bit lax or if you have habitual neck tension or less than perfect posture. Take a moment to get in touch with your body and feel the support of the hard surface beneath you.

LEVEL UP

- Opt for a more expansive stretch through your body by opening your arms and legs wider. Knit your ribcage closed and press the middle of your back gently down into the floor beneath you. Breathe deeply here for 45 to 60 seconds.

REMEMBER:

As much as you'd like to relax in this pose, keep your shoulders from creeping up toward your neck. Allow the top of your head to pull away from your chest to help create space along the back of your neck.

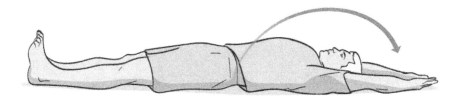

Instructions:

1. Find an area, preferably a hard surface, where you can safely lie down with your arms and legs fully extended.
2. Lie down with your arms at your sides with your palms facing up. Then, keeping your arms on the floor, slowly extend your arms overhead and at a slight diagonal.
3. Slide your feet open to more than hip-width apart, forming an X with your body.
4. Create opposition in your stretch by imagining your arms and legs pulling away from your torso.
5. Hold for 30 to 60 seconds.

Arm Circles

AFFECTED AREAS

- Shoulders: deltoids
- Upper back: trapezius, rhomboids
- Rotator cuffs

GOOD FOR

- Arm circles allow you to get your energy flowing while expanding a full range of movement that begins from inside the shoulder rotators. If you feel tight in your neck and shoulders, this dynamic stretch will help release pent-up tension in those areas.

LEVEL UP

- Sweep your arms around in larger circles for an added challenge and more expansion through your chest. Try holding light weights or using weighted wrist cuffs when you're more advanced.

REMEMBER:

Proper breathing during this exercise will give you greater results. Although this is a dynamic stretch, keep your torso steady and control the movement to prevent pulling a muscle.

Instructions:

1. Begin by standing with your feet hip-width apart and your arms hanging loosely at your sides.
2. Bring your arms up and out to your sides in one graceful sweep, keeping your elbows straight.
3. Slowly rotate your arms forward and circle them down and around, forming small circles.
4. Repeat a series of five circles, and repeat in the opposite direction.

Shoulder Hyperextension

AFFECTED AREAS

- Upper back: trapezius
- Shoulders: deltoids
- Forearms
- Wrists

GOOD FOR

- Performing repetitive tasks, whether at work or at home, often involves asymmetric movement patterns that can eventually cause parts of your body to hold tension and create discomfort. This elbow inversion relieves tightness around your shoulders and arms in a whole new way.

LEVEL UP

- This move is already quite intense; however, if you'd like more of a challenge, make your hands into fists, and work toward bringing your fists to touch behind the middle of your back, then imagine bringing your elbows forward.

REMEMBER:

As soon as you feel a stretch, at whatever point that is for you, stop there and breathe. Don't push too hard in this stretch.

Instructions:

1. Find a comfortable position, either standing or seated.
2. Lengthen your back, and place the tops of your hands high on your waist.
3. Slowly slide your fingers and wrists back behind your lower ribcage.
4. Gently rotate your shoulders and elbows forward. Elongate your neck, and keep your shoulders soft as your shoulders slide forward.
5. Hold for 30 to 60 seconds, and repeat three times.

Shoulder Circles

AFFECTED AREAS

- Upper back: trapezius
- Chest: pectorals
- Shoulders: deltoids

GOOD FOR

- Sometimes the smallest movements can have the greatest impact. When you have a moment of peace, close your eyes and allow this stretch to melt away pent-up tension in your upper body. Perform these shoulder circles as big or as small as you'd like.

LEVEL UP

- Expand the stretch into the sides of your neck by isolating one shoulder at a time. Lean your right ear toward your right shoulder as you circle your left shoulder. Then lean your left ear toward your left shoulder as you circle your right shoulder.

ON THE FLY

- This is a very effective stress-relieving stretch that can be done multiple times a day. And you can take it with you anywhere you go.

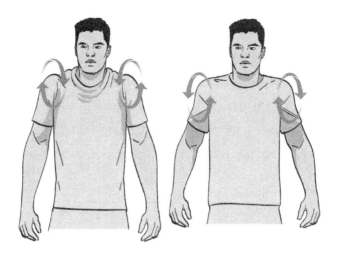

Instructions:

1. Find a comfortable position, either standing or seated.
2. Relax arms and shoulders.
3. Slowly rotate your shoulders from front to back.
4. Roll them 10 times from front to back and then 10 more times from back to front. Repeat three times.

Arms, Wrists and Hands

The arms and the wrists and hands are the versatile work-horses of the body—performing feats of physical strength and detailed maneuvers. Arm stretches also benefit the delicate mechanisms of the wrists and hands by strengthening them against injury and relieving stiffness and pain.

Wall-Assisted Bicep Stretch

AFFECTED AREAS

- Shoulders: deltoids
- Chest: upper pectorals
- Upper arms: biceps
- Forearms: brachialis

GOOD FOR

- This simple wall-assisted stretch lengthens the muscles along your chest, down your arms, and into your wrists. Find soothing relief from tight chest muscles and stiff shoulders and arms.

LEVEL UP

- For a more intense opening along the back of your neck, slowly turn your head away from the wall to look toward the opposite shoulder.

REMEMBER:

Root down through your legs and engage your core muscles to fully support your weight from your center.

Try not to tense up your shoulders.

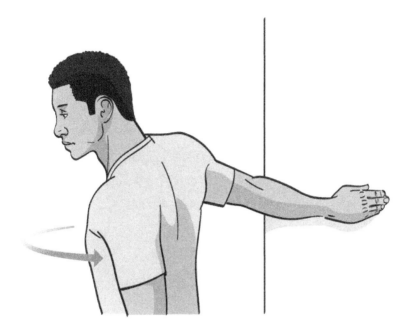

Instructions:

- Stand with your right side about a foot away from a wall.
- Step your left foot forward into an open stance.
- Extend your right arm to shoulder height, and rest the palm of your hand on the wall above you.
- Keeping contact with the wall, allow your right arm to slowly circle back and down behind you, bringing your hand to rest just below shoulder height.
- Open your chest and bend your left knee slightly, shifting your weight several inches forward.
- Inhale and exhale deeply as you hold here for 15 to 30 seconds.
- Switch sides and repeat three times on each arm.

Tricep Stretch

AFFECTED AREAS

- Upper arms: triceps, biceps
- Shoulders: deltoids

GOOD FOR

- Counterbalance the downward pull of gravity on your arms by lifting your arms overhead and lengthening the sides of your body. As a result, you'll be able to loosen the area along the back of your arms and find some solace from tight shoulders.

LEVEL UP

- Throw in the towel to ramp up this stretch. Grab one end of a rolled-up towel with your raised arm. Bring your opposite hand to your lower back and gently pull on the towel for 15 to 30 seconds.

REMEMBER:

Try to engage your core muscles and open your chest as you perform this exercise. Keep your back straight throughout.

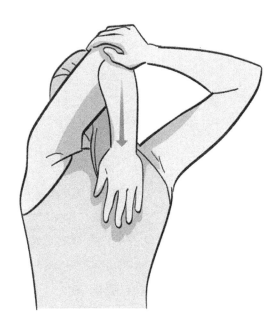

Instructions:

- Find a comfortable stance or a supported seated position.
- Raise your left arm straight up along your left ear.
- Turn your arm inward so that your palm is facing behind you.
- Bring your right hand up to support your left elbow as you slowly bend your left elbow, reaching your palm to the back of your left shoulder.
- Use your right hand to gently press your left elbow up and back for a stretch. Hold for 20 seconds at the top of the move and breathe.
- Repeat three to four times.

Wrist Flexion

AFFECTED AREAS

- Upper arms: biceps
- Forearms: pronators, extensors, wrist flexors

GOOD FOR

- If your daily routine involves a lot of work with your hands or you have a hobby such as weight lifting, tennis, cooking, sewing, or gardening, this simple dynamic stretch will provide extensive relief through your wrists, forearms, and fingers.

LEVEL UP

- Intensify the stretch by curling your extended fingers into a downward-facing fist. While keeping light pressure on the back of your wrist with your supporting hand, gently pull your fist down and away from your wrist.

REMEMBER:

The shoulder of the extended arm will naturally want to lift, but try to keep both shoulders square and relaxed. Imagine pulling your shoulder blades down your back.

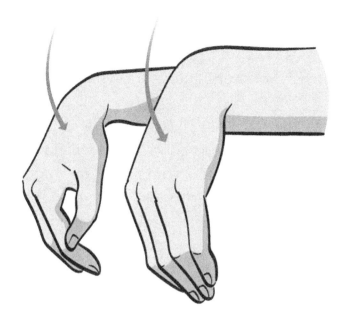

Instructions:

1. Begin either standing or seated and extend your left arm straight out in front of you.
2. Press your left fingers and thumb together, and flex your wrist downward, pointing your fingers toward the floor.
3. With your right hand, gently press your left fingers, bringing them closer to your body.
4. Hold for 15 to 30 seconds, and repeat three to four times.

Wrist Extension

AFFECTED AREAS

- Forearms: pronators, extensors, wrist flexors

GOOD FOR

- Your wrists and hands control and facilitate multiple daily tasks. Additionally, your hands rarely get a break for very long with the onset of texting. Ease away painful wrist tension and hand cramping with this stretch—a little extension goes a long way.

LEVEL UP

- Hold your arm in place for an additional challenge and slowly bend and straighten your extended elbow while keeping light pressure on your palm with the supporting hand.

REMEMBER:

It might surprise you how much stretch you feel with this simple move. You need only apply light pressure from your supporting hand to achieve a maximum stretch.

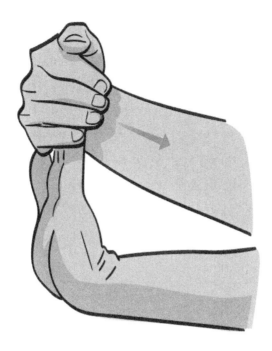

Instructions:

- Begin seated or standing, and extend your right arm straight out in front of you, palm facing down.
- Press your right fingers and thumb together, and pivot your wrist upward, pointing your fingers toward the ceiling.
- Stretch from the base of your wrist as you bring your left hand to your right fingers.
- With your left hand, gently press your right fingers back.
- Hold for 15 to 30 seconds, and repeat three times on each wrist.

Core and Hips

Core stretches benefit a group of critical muscles, toning your abdominals along the front and sides of your torso. These stretches improve your balance and sports performance. Hip stretches are also essential for maintaining proper balance and coordination. By performing core and hip stretches regularly, you'll improve the range of motion in your lower body and help protect against injuries.

Hip Twist

AFFECTED AREAS

- Buttocks: gluteals
- Hip rotators: piriformis, quadratus femoris
- Abdomen: abdominal obliques, transverse abdominus

GOOD FOR

- Open those hard-to-reach muscles that wrap across your lower back and hips and along the sides of your torso. The twisting movement of this stretch helps improve posture and lower-back pain.

LEVEL UP

- Intensify this twisted movement by pushing down strongly into your right hand. Lift your core up and in, and straighten your left arm, reaching your left fingertips down to the floor.

ON THE FLY

- If you find it challenging to sit up straight through your lower spine in this pose, place a rolled-up towel, yoga block, or firm pillow under your hips for support.

Instructions:

1. Sit with your legs extended in front of you.
2. Step your left foot over your right knee, and rest your left foot on the floor just outside your right knee.
3. Place your left hand on the floor near your left hip, and put weight on it for support.
4. Raise your right arm, pull in your abs, and root your left foot down. Lengthen through your spine as you twist your torso to your left.
5. Lower your right arm. Bend your right elbow, and place it on the outside of your left knee.
6. Push down into your left arm and twist your upper torso, turning your head to look to your left.
7. Hold for 20 to 30 seconds, and repeat three times on each side.

Cobra

AFFECTED AREAS

- Abdomen: rectus abdominus, abdominal obliques
- Chest: pectorals
- Back: erector spinae
- Hip flexors: psoas

GOOD FOR

- A sedentary lifestyle can be detrimental to the health of your hips and core, weakening the muscles that support your upper and lower body. Try the Cobra to alleviate tightness in the front of your hips and to counteract slouching and a tucked-in pelvis.

LEVEL UP

- Once you're confident with the basic Cobra, intensify the stretch. Begin in the same position, except bring your hands slightly farther down from your shoulders toward your chest. Push into your hands, and lift your body a little higher.

REMEMBER:

To protect your lower back during this upward movement, be sure to activate your lower abdominals. Before you push down into your hands to lift your body, squeeze in those abs and keep them tight.

Instructions:

1. Lie face down on the floor with your legs extended straight behind you and your feet about shoulder-width apart.
2. Press your forearms to the floor at the sides of your head.
3. Strongly pull in your core, and push down into your hands as you slowly lift your upper body from the floor. Rise only as far as is comfortable.
4. Roll your shoulders back and try to straighten your arms.
5. Point your toes and keep the tops of your feet in contact with the floor.
6. Lift your chin, open your chest, and gaze slightly upward
7. Hold for 20 to 30 seconds and breathe deeply. Repeat three times.

Butterfly

AFFECTED AREAS

- Inner thighs: adductors
- Hips: abductors
- Buttocks: gluteals

GOOD FOR

- The Butterfly is a great hip flexor stretch for everyone, from athletes to office workers. Allow gravity to assist you in opening your hips and inner thighs as you lower your knees out to your sides. By keeping your hips limber, you'll also help protect against groin injuries.

LEVEL UP

- When you're ready for more of a challenge, pull in your feet closer to your groin and hold your ankles. Push gently on your legs with your forearms to lower your knees farther toward the floor and bow your head toward your feet.

REMEMBER:

If your hips are very tight or you are struggling to sit on the floor with a straight back, add some support by tucking a folded towel or a small yoga block under your hips.

Instructions:

- Take a moment to find a comfortable place to sit on a firm surface. Extend your legs out in front of you, and support your body by placing your hands at the sides of your hips.
- Bend your knees, turning your legs outward.
- Reach forward, place your hands on your ankles, and press the soles of your feet together.
- Pull in your abdominals and lengthen through your lower back. Allow your knees to drop open and down with the pull of gravity.
- Breathe deeply and hold for 20 to 30 seconds.
- Repeat three times.

Flexor Stretch

AFFECTED AREAS

- Hip flexors: psoas, iliacus, sartorius
- Thighs: quadriceps, hamstrings, adductors

GOOD FOR

- This stretch reaches deep into your hips and opens the muscles around the front and back of your pelvis while lengthening your core. Because this stretch requires a deep folding in your hips, you should be thoroughly warmed up in your back, hips, and legs.

LEVEL UP

- Give yourself a deeper stretch by keeping both legs straight. Begin standing and step your left foot far forward. Lean your torso forward, and lower your hands to the floor on either side of your left foot. Flex your left foot and hold for up to 30 seconds.

REMEMBER:

Be sure to keep your hips square rather than shifted to one side. Relax your neck and shoulders as you lean forward.

Instructions:

1. Begin by kneeling on the floor with the tops of your feet touching the floor.
2. Extend your left leg forward and place your left foot on the floor, keeping a slight bend in your knee.
3. Raise your arms overhead, keep your back straight, and find your balance.
4. Next, flex your extended left foot and lean your torso forward. Finally, lower your hands to the floor at your sides for balance.
5. Hold for 20 seconds and repeat on the opposite side.
6. Perform three sets.

Alternate Hip Internal Rotation

AFFECTED AREAS

- Buttocks: piriformis, gluteus minimus
- Thighs: adductors, abductors
- Lower back: psoas, erector spinae

GOOD FOR

- Internally rotating the hips is a great way to counterbalance all the outward hip movements that we perform daily such as walking, sitting, and standing. In addition, this stretch improves flexibility through your hips and pelvis while opening the hard-to-reach areas of your lower back.

LEVEL UP

- With your legs wide and feet flat on the floor, let both knees drop together to your right side in a controlled manner. Then, return to the starting position and lower your legs to your left. Perform 10 repetitions.

REMEMBER:

Engage your abs the entire time. Breathe deeply as you perform this movement slowly and deliberately.

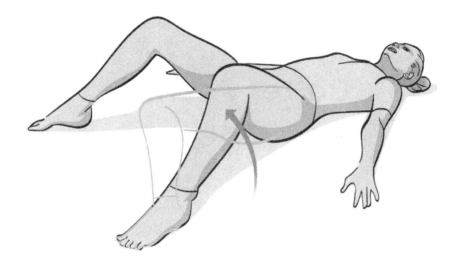

Instructions:

1. Lie on your back with your knees bent at about 90° and your feet shoulder-width apart.
2. Extend your arms out to your sides, and press your palms to the floor. Slowly lower your left knee toward the floor, allowing your left foot to rotate inward and return to the starting position.
3. Lower your right knee and return to the starting position.
4. Repeat 10 times on each side.

Chapter 6

Stretching for a Better Posture

You can work on your natural posture even during everyday tasks like brushing your teeth or standing at your kitchen counter. Explore these mindful movement sequences in the comfort of your own home throughout your day, and notice how much your posture begins to improve.

Wake-Up Stretch

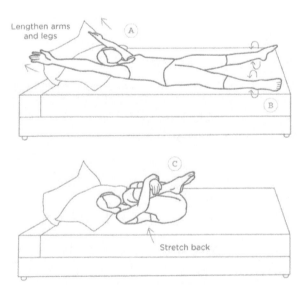

Effects: Stimulates your nervous system, lubricates your joints, and gets your blood flowing.

Equipment: A bed.

1. Take three deep breaths and visualize moving through your day with ease when you wake up. Stretch your arms and legs away from each other in a big X, Ⓐ and circle your wrists and ankles. Ⓑ

2. Hug your knees into your chest, Ⓒ and stretch your back.

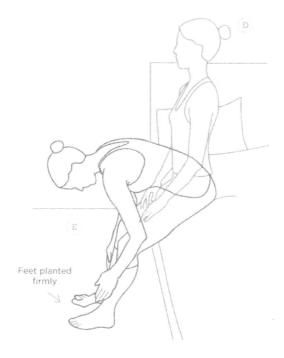

Feet planted firmly

3. Roll up into a neutral seated position Ⓓ on the side of your bed with your feet flat on the floor.

4. Using both hands, gently perform a series of taps down the front, back, and sides of your legs to your

feet, 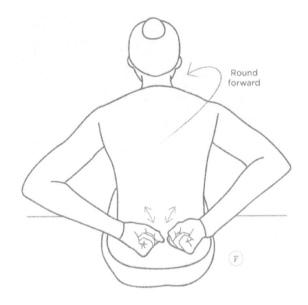 then tap back up to your chest and shoulders and brush your fingers down your arms.

Round forward

5. Round forward and gently pound both sides of your lower back with a soft fist. Ⓕ
6. Elongate your back and return to a neutral seated position, Ⓓ noticing your effortlessly natural posture.

TIP: Set your alarm five minutes early so you'll have time to start your day with this stretch.

Shower Stretch

TIPS: Shoulders and knees stay soft and relaxed. Be careful not to slip. Avoid this exercise if you have glaucoma, high or low blood pressure, or acute shoulder pain.

Effects: Decompresses and articulates your spine, and stretches your hamstrings.

Equipment: A shower or wall.

1. With the water running, stand facing away from the showerhead and look toward the wall in front of you.
2. Slide your hands up the wall as your shoulder blades slide down. Ⓐ Keeping your shoulders down, reach a little farther up with your hands, drawing your ribs away from your pelvis. Take three deep breaths as you decompress your spine.

3. Keeping the length in your spine, step away from the wall Ⓑ and stand facing away from the showerhead, so the warm water is flowing down your back.

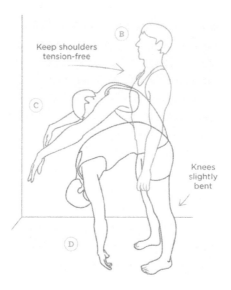

Keep shoulders
tension-free

Knees
slightly
bent

4. Begin to slowly roll your spine forward, one vertebra at a time. Ⓒ Nod your chin to your chest, soften your sternum and curl over your heart, ribs, and belly button. With your knees slightly bent, reach gently toward your feet, stretching your hamstrings. Ⓓ
5. Take a deep breath and visualize your back filling up with air like a parachute
6. Pushing down through your legs, slowly roll back up through your spine to a standing position. Ⓑ

Pelvic Clock

TIPS: Move slowly without tension and breathe. Initiate the movement from your pelvis. Stabilize your legs and hips, and keep hip flexors and glutes relaxed. Avoid this exercise if you have acute back pain.

Effects: Helps you find and maintain the integrity of your spinal curves, warms up your lower back and pelvic floor muscles, and enhances pelvic mobility.

Equipment: A mat and a pillow or towel (optional).

1. Lie on your back with your knees bent, your feet flat on the floor, and your arms by your sides. Use a pillow under your neck or lower back for support if needed. Your lower back should have a soft, natural arch. (Imagine a few ladybugs being able to crawl through.)

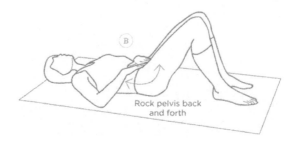

Rock pelvis back
and forth

2. Place your hands on your pelvis, reaching your fingers toward your pubic bone and your thumbs toward your belly button. (A) The triangle of your hands
   should be horizontally level. Imagine resting a drink
   on your lower abs and not spilling it. Your ribs should
   be softening down toward your belly button and an-
   choring you into the ground. This is the neutral position.

3. With your hands still in the triangle, create an arch by
   rocking your pelvis toward your fingers/pubic bone.
   (B) The move is very small. Then rock back toward
   your thumbs/belly button. Rock back and forth eight
   times, breathing naturally. Finish in neutral. Notice
   how your back feels.

4. Next, imagine a clock face on your pelvis. Trace a circle with your pelvis, connecting all the numbers from
   1 through 12. Feel your back stretching and lengthening.

Kitchen Counter Stretch

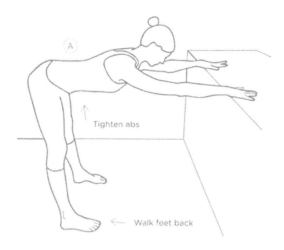

Effects: Stretches your hip flexors and hamstrings, increases your hip mobility and extends your spine.

Equipment: A kitchen counter.

1. In a standing position, place both hands on the counter in front of you, shoulder-distance apart.
2. Walk your feet back as you fold forward from your hips so that your body forms an upside-down L, with your chest and head slightly above your shoulders in line with your spine. Ⓐ Keep your spine elongated and engage your core.

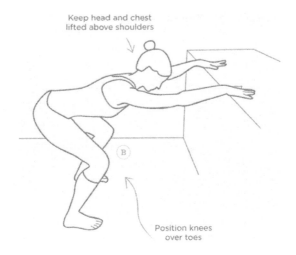

3. Keeping your knees aligned over your big toes, inhale as you bend your knees Ⓑ and exhale as you straighten them. Repeat five times.

4. **TIPS:** Don't drop your chest and head below your shoulders or hyperextend your knees, and don't forget to use your core. Avoid this exercise if you have shoulder and hip injuries.

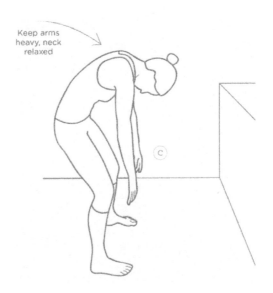

5. Soften your knees, remove your hands from the counter, Ⓒ and slowly roll back up.

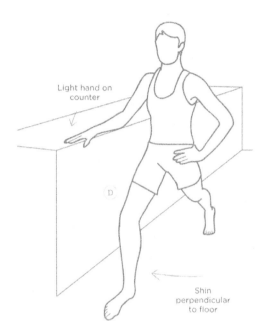

6. Turn to the side with your right hand on the counter for balance. Step forward into a lunge with your right leg. Keeping your right knee bent, reach through your left heel while keeping your left leg as straight as possible. Ⓓ

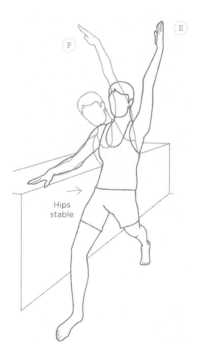

7. Reach your left arm up toward the ceiling, pulling in your abs and pushing your outside hip forward so that it's square with your inside hip and shoulders. Try reaching toward the counter for an extra side stretch (optional).

8. Hold for five deep breaths.

9. Repeat steps 5 through 7 on the other side.

Cat-Cow, Bird Dog Sequence

Effects: Improves your balance, coordination, and sense of where you are in space; strengthens your spine and core.

Equipment: A mat.

1. Get down on your hands and knees on a mat, with your wrists directly under your shoulders and your knees directly below your hips. Ⓐ This is the neutral position.
2. Pointing your nose toward your pubic bone, round your spine upward like a cat arching its back. Ⓑ (This is the "cat" portion of the cat-cow.)

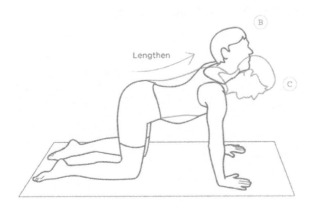

3. Now stretch your spine in the opposite direction, arching it toward the floor as you reach the crown of your head toward your tailbone. Ⓑ Soften your elbows. (This is the "cow" portion of the cat-cow.)

4. Return to a relaxed all-fours position with your spine neutral like a table. Ⓒ Spread your fingers and distribute your weight evenly over your hands. Press the floor away as you engage your back and chest muscles to stabilize your shoulders.

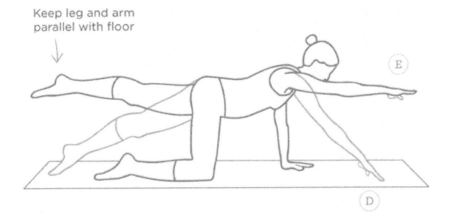

5. Inhale and straighten your right arm out forward and your left leg out backward until they're touching the floor with just the fingertips and toes. (D)

6. Exhale, and, using your core, lift your right arm and left leg straight up in line with your hip and shoulder joints until they're parallel with the floor. (E) (This is the "bird dog" because it makes you look like an alert hunting dog.)

7. Repeat steps 4 through 6 using your left arm and right leg.

8. Perform three sets of the whole sequence, from cat-cow to bird dog.

TIPS: During the bird dog, keep your head, arm, and leg aligned with your spine. Engage your core so your lower back doesn't arch. Avoid this sequence if you have knee or wrist injuries.

Chapter 7

Warm-Up Stretches

Warming up before doing an activity gets your body and muscles ready for action. Just like you warm up a car in cold weather by starting it and letting it heat up to get the fluids moving, it's important to warm up your body to raise your body temperature and get the blood flowing to your muscles. You may be inclined to skip any kind of warm-up in order to get straight to your workout or activity, but you will be missing out on a crucial step and possibly jeopardizing yourself for injury. So what are the benefits of warming up and stretching prior to a cardio workout, weight lifting, or sports activity? According to Cronkleton (2019), the benefits include:

- Lessened risk of injury because muscles are relaxed.
- Increased flexibility and ease of movement. Increased range of motion also reduces stress on joints and the tendons that support them.
- Decreased muscle stiffness because muscles are warmed up.
- Greater oxygen and blood flow throughout your body and muscles because your body temperature has risen while warming up and stretching.

Most of us know to warm up before exercising at home or at the gym, but what about other activities? It's important for the muscles to be warmed up prior to every day activities such as biking, bowling, dancing, gardening, team sports, and even sex. Warming up by gradually increasing your heart rate and breathing allows your body to acclimate to the activity that it will soon be doing.

What is the best way to warm up and stretch prior to our activity? The American Heart Association (2014) recommends the following:

- Walk for five to ten minutes to get the muscles warmed up. An alternative would be to ride a stationary bike or swim for the same amount of time.
- Gradually proceed into your workout by doing whatever you plan on doing for exercise, but at a slower pace. If you are going to run, start off by jogging slowly.
- Incorporate movement into your stretches, but do not bounce. Instead, stretch your entire body, both upper and lower areas.

Don't feel you have to do all the stretches listed in this chapter before your intended activity. Pick a few upper body and a few lower body stretches and do those. Next time, change it up and pick different ones to do.

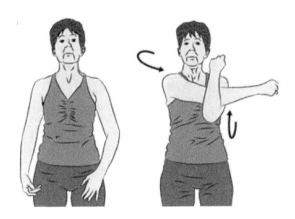

Upper Body Stretches

Cross Body Shoulder Stretch

Areas stretched: shoulders, upper back

Instructions:

1. Stand up tall with feet about hip-width apart.
2. Bring your left arm up and across your chest to the right side. Support your arm by bending your right arm and letting your left forearm rest in the inside crook of your elbow. Take a deep breath in and then exhale. Return arms to your sides.
3. Next, bring your right arm up and across your chest to the left side. Let your right forearm rest in the inside crook of your other elbow. Breathe in and out. Return arms to your side.
4. Repeat stretches for both arms two or three more times.

Take note:

- Alternate support for the arm that is being stretched: stand facing a wall and allow your arm that is crossing your chest to rest between your chest and the wall.
- You can also do this stretch while sitting.

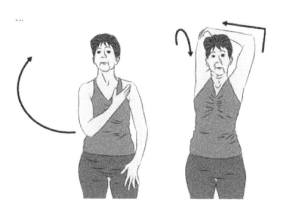

Overhead Tricep Stretch

Areas stretched: triceps.

Instructions:

1. Stand up tall with your feet about hip-width apart. Shrug your shoulders up and then down.
2. Raise your left hand and arm above your head. Bend your left arm and place your left hand on the back of your neck or spine. Use your right hand to gently push your left elbow back as you slide your hand further down, if possible. Take a deep breath in and then

exhale. Hold the position for two more breaths in and out. Return the left arm back down to your side.

3. Stretch the other arm by bringing your right hand and arm above your head. Bend the right arm and bring your hand to the back of your neck or spine. Use the other hand to push the right elbow back as your hand reaches further down. Take a deep breath in and then exhale. Hold the position for two more breaths in and out. Return the right arm back down to your side.

4. Repeat the stretch on each arm if desired.

Take note:

- Be sure to keep your hips tucked under you, so you don't sway and arch out in your lower back. This stretch can also be done while seated.

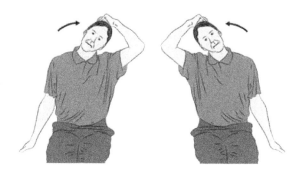

Ear to Shoulder Neck Stretch

Areas stretched: sides of the neck, tops of shoulders.

Instructions:

1. From a standing or sitting position, look straight ahead and relax the shoulders. Then, shrug the shoulders up and then down.
2. While looking straight ahead, gently tilt the head, so the left ear moves towards the top of the left shoulder. Take a deep breath in and then exhale.
3. Gently turn your head so you are now looking at your left armpit. Take a deep breath in and then exhale. Then, slowly return the head upright.
4. Look straight ahead and gently tilt the head to the right to stretch the other side. Your right ear will move towards the top of your right shoulder. Take a deep breath and exhale.
5. Gently turn your head so your gaze now is towards your right armpit. Take a deep breath in and then exhale. Then, slowly return the head upright.

Take note:

- It's important to be very gentle and careful with your neck, especially if you have any neck problems or pain. Do this stretch slowly and deliberately, pausing when you need to. Skip that part if looking down towards your armpit is too much for your neck.

Standing Chest Stretch

Areas stretched: chest muscles, front of shoulders.

Instructions:

1. Stand up tall with feet, hip-width apart, and arms at your sides.

2. Bring your hands behind you, clasp them together, and rest them on your lower back. As you take a breath in, push your chest out as you raise your clasped hands off your lower back and further out

behind you. Exhale slowly. Hold the position for two more deep inhales and exhales.

3. Return hands to starting position. Repeat the stretch two or three more times if desired.

Take note:

- Be sure you do not scrunch up your shoulders as you do this stretch. They should be down and away from your ears and your neck should be kept long and relaxed.

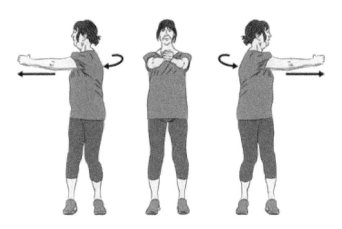

Standing Torso Twist

Areas stretched: abdominals, obliques, spine.

Instructions:

1. With feet about hip-width apart, stand up tall with arms at your sides. Lift your arms up and out from your sides to form a T-shape. Take a deep breath in.
2. As you exhale, gently and slowly twist your upper body, including your head and arms, to the left. You

should be looking to the left, and your lower body and hips are still straight ahead. Hold the position and breathe in and out. Return to the starting position.

3. To stretch the other side, breath in as you lift your arms up and out to a T-shape. Exhaling, gently twist your upper body, head, and arms to the right. Again, your hips should still be facing forward and your head should be looking right. Breathe in and out as you hold the position. Return to the starting position.

4. Repeat stretches on both sides two or three more times.

Take note:

- Don't be aggressive or jerky as you twist to the left or right. Instead, protect your back and spine by moving slowly and gently.
- An alternate arm position is to bend your arms and bring your fingertips to the top of your shoulders as you twist.

Lower Body Stretches

Hurdler Hamstring Stretch

Areas stretched: hamstrings, glutes, hips.

Instructions:

1. Sit on the floor with both legs out straight in front of you. Bend your left leg and bring your foot to the inside of your calf, knee, or thigh.
2. Raise both arms overhead and take a deep breath in. Bend forward at the hip and bring your arms and torso down towards your knee as you exhale. Depending on your flexibility, you may or may not be able to touch the floor in front of you. Take a deep breath in and exhale. Hold this position for two more breaths in and out. Then, raise the torso and come back up to the starting position.
3. Switch legs by now, bending your right leg and bringing your right foot to the inside of your calf, knee, or thigh.
4. Raise both arms and breathe in. Bend forward towards your knee as you exhale and reach for the floor. Hold this position for two more breaths in and out.

Return to the starting position. Repeat the stretch on each side two more times.

Take note:

- Remember, don't bounce while doing this stretch, and don't force your torso down. Only bend as far as is comfortable for your hamstrings.

Standing Calf Stretch

Areas stretched: calves.

Instructions:

1. Standing up tall with feet about 12 to 24 inches away from a wall or sturdy chair, place both hands on the wall or chair.
2. Lift the left foot and step it back into a mini lunge while slightly bending the right leg. Press your hands against the wall while you bring your left heel down to the floor, if possible. Take a deep breath in and slowly exhale. Bend your left leg to lift the heel off the floor, and then try pushing the

heel down to the floor again. Return to the starting position.

3. To stretch the other leg, lift the right foot and step back into a mini lunge while slightly bending the other leg. Press your hands against the wall as you bring your right heel down to the floor. Breath in and out. Bend your right leg, lift the heel off the floor, and then push the heel down again. Return to the starting position. Repeat the stretch on both sides two more times.

Take note:

- Your heel might not touch the floor, and that is okay. The goal here is to stretch your calf muscles to a comfortable point.

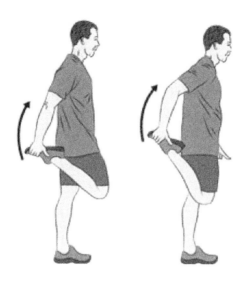

Quad Stretch

Areas stretched: quads, front of hips.

Instructions:

1. Stand up tall with both feet on the ground. If you need help balancing, you can place one hand on the wall or on the back of a sturdy chair.

2. Bend your left leg behind you and grab your left ankle with your left hand. Bring your heel as close to your glutes as you can without forcing or straining. Take a deep breath in and then exhale. Bring the leg back down to starting position.

3. To stretch the other leg, bend your right leg behind you. Grab your right ankle with your right hand and bring your heel to your glutes as close as possible. Breathe in and out. Bring the leg back down to starting position.

4. Repeat stretches on both legs two more times.

Take note:

*   Be sure that you don't allow your lower back to arch. Keep the hips tucked under and the pelvis facing forward.
*   If you cannot do this stretch while standing, you can do it while lying on the floor. Laying on your left side, use your right hand to grab your right ankle. Then, lay on your other side to do the other leg.

Seated Butterfly

Areas stretched: inner thighs, groin, hips, knees.

Instructions:

1. Sit up tall on the floor with your legs straight out in front of you. Bend your knees out to either side and bring the soles of both feet together.

2. Slide both feet towards you as far as you can, keeping their soles touching. Depending on your flexibility, your knees may be either high off the ground or nearly touching the floor, so your legs make the shape of butterfly wings.

3. Take a deep breath in. While you exhale, bend forward and bring your hands to the ground in front of you as you lean forward slowly. Again, depending on the openness of your hips, you may or may not be able to touch the ground with your hands or lean very far forward. Breathe in and out two more times in this position.

4. Return to the starting position. Do this stretch two more times.

Take note:

- If you are able, you can deepen the stretch by allowing your elbows to gently press down on your thighs as you are leaning forward.

- Don't round your back as you lean forward. Instead, keep your spine straight, your neck long, and your gaze downwards.

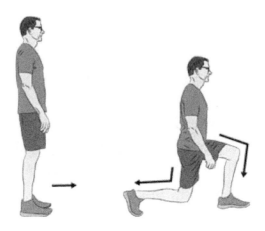

Standing Lunge

Areas stretched: hip flexors, quads, calves.

Instructions:

1. Stand up tall with your feet, hip-width apart. You can stand next to a wall or sturdy chair for support for stability and balance.

2. Step back with your left foot behind you and bend your right knee. Your right knee should be directly over your right foot and bent at a 90° angle. Keep your torso upright, and do not lean forward. You should feel the stretch in the front of your left hip. Take a deep breath in and then exhale. Hold the position for two more breaths. Return feet to starting position.

3. To stretch the other leg, step back with your right foot while bending your other knee. Now you should feel the stretch in the front of your right hip. Breathe deep in and then out. Hold the position for two more

breaths. Return feet to starting position. Repeat the stretch two more times on each side.

Take note:

- Do not lean forward during this stretch. Keep your body upright, and your pelvis pushed forward to ensure that your hip flexor is engaged and being stretched.
- Remember to keep your knee behind your toes so it stays at a 90° angle. Letting the knee come forward past your toes puts unnecessary stress on your knee.

Chapter 8

Post-Workout Stretches

When we exercise or participate in an activity that gets our heart rate up, our blood is pumping, and our blood vessels are dilated to deliver blood and oxygen to our muscles. Stretching and cooling down after participating in an activity is important to bring your body back to a normal state. Stopping suddenly after exercising or strenuous activity can cause your blood pressure and heart rate to plummet and make you feel as if you will pass out. Coming to a sudden stop can cause a feeling of sickness and lightheadedness. Gradual cessation of activity helps the body shift to decreased movement and exertion.

It is beneficial to stretch when the body is cooling down after exercise or prolonged activity. Muscles are still warm, as are joints and tendons. Stretching while still warm allows the muscles to stretch further and deeper, leading to increased flexibility and mobility. It is also good to stretch after activity to prevent lactic acid build-up in the muscles. Lactic acid builds up in muscles when there is not enough oxygen getting to the muscles. The result is stiffness and soreness in the muscles that can last for days. Stretching and drinking plenty of water help prevent lactic acid build-up (Cronkleton, 2018) by encouraging circulation and relieving muscle tension.

What is the best way to cool down and stretch post-activity? According to the American Heart Association (2014), you should:

- Walk until your heart rate comes down (ideally below 120 beats per minute), about five minutes.
- Stretch the entire body, both upper and lower, and hold stretches for several breaths, about 30 seconds.
- Stretch deeply but not to the point of pain. Never bounce while stretching.

Cooling down and stretching after exercise and activity allow our bodies to recover. Our heart rate and blood pressure gradually return to what they were before we started our activity. Stretching while muscles are warm also prevents the blood from pooling in our lower body or other extremities after exercising. Plus, stretching after exercise or any activity feels good!

Upper Body Stretches

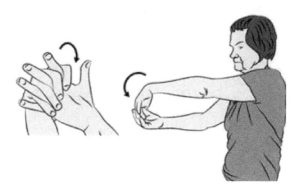

Wrist Rotation Bicep Stretch

Areas stretched: biceps, thumb, shoulder.

Instructions:

1. Stand up tall with your feet about hip-width apart. Raise your arms out and away from your sides into a T position.
2. With your palms facing forward, make each hand into a fist leaving the thumb free and pointed up. You will be making the "thumbs up" sign with both hands! Take a deep breath in and then exhale.
3. Now, rotate your wrists and arms so that your thumbs are pointing towards the floor. You will now be making the "thumbs down" sign with both hands. Breath in and out.
4. Repeat the stretch two or three more times, going from thumbs up to thumbs down slowly and breathing naturally.

Take note:

- Don't let your shoulders round, and don't let your chest collapse inwards while doing this stretch. Keep your chest out and pushed forward for good posture.
- You can do this stretch while seated.

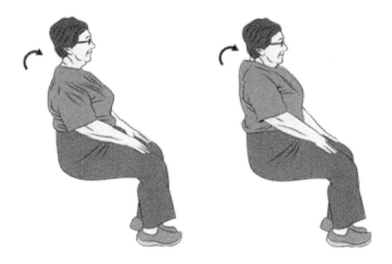

Shoulder Rolls

Areas stretched: shoulders, including trapezius muscles.

Instructions:

1. Stand tall with feet about hip-width apart and arms hanging down by your sides.
2. Slowly raise your shoulders towards your ears and then roll them back, squeezing your shoulder blades together. Breathing naturally, roll the shoulders up and back three to five more times. Return shoulders to the starting position.

3. Now roll the shoulders the other way by slowly raising them up towards your ears and roll them forward while rounding your upper back. Breathe naturally and continue to roll the shoulders up and forward three to five more times. Return shoulders to the starting position.

Take note:

- This stretch can be done any time your neck and shoulders are starting to feel tense. You can also do this stretch while sitting.

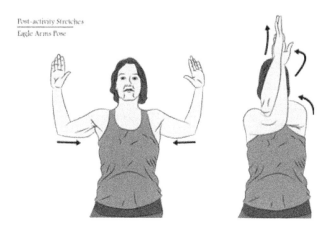

Post-activity Stretches
Eagle Arms Pose

Eagle Arms Pose

Areas stretched: shoulders, upper back, triceps.

Instructions:

1. From a standing or sitting position, bring both arms out in front of you and bend them so the elbows form a 90° angle.
2. Cross the forearms so that the right elbow is under the left elbow and the backs of your hands are touching each other. Raise your arms so that your elbows are about shoulder height. Take a deep breath in and then exhale. You should feel this stretch all across your upper back and shoulders. Slowly uncross your forearms and return your arms to your sides.
3. To stretch the other way, bring your arms out in front of you and bend them again. Cross forearms this time so that your left elbow is under your right one. Raise your elbows to about shoulder height and breathe

deeply in and out. Slowly uncross your forearms and return your arms to your sides.

4. Repeat this stretch two or three more times.

Take note:

- Depending on the size of your arms and your chest, you may or may not be able to cross your forearms and get one elbow under the other. However, it is perfectly okay just to bring the forearms together and raise your elbows to shoulder height.
- Be sure to keep your shoulders down and away from your ears. Don't scrunch up!
- If you want to deepen the stretch, instead of just the backs of your hands touching each other, do another cross at the wrists and try to get your palms to touch each other.

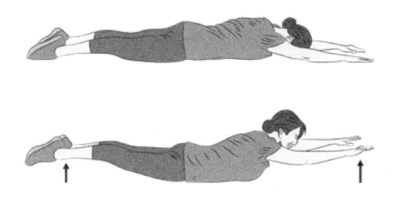

Superman Stretch

Areas stretched: upper back, shoulders, abdominals, spinal muscles, lower back, glutes.

Instructions:

1. Lie on the floor, face and belly down, with arms out in front of you and legs straight.
2. Take a deep breath in and slowly raise your arms and legs off the floor a few inches and draw in your belly button. You should feel a contraction in your lower back, and your body should look as if you are flying through the air like a superhero! Exhale and slowly lower your arms and legs to the ground.
3. Repeat the stretch two or three more times.

Take note:

*   Keep your neck straight and look down at the ground, not straight ahead of you, as that will put too much pressure on the neck.

- Lift your arms and legs only to where it is comfortable. If lifting both is too hard, just raise your arms.

Lying Pectoral Stretch

Areas stretched: pectoral and chest muscles.

Instructions:

1. Lie on the floor, face and belly down. Legs should be straight, and arms extended straight out to the sides away from your body.
2. Bend your left arm and bring your left hand to the floor just under your left shoulder. Take a deep breath in, and while exhaling, push into your left hand as you roll onto your right hip. Keep your right arm straight and extended out. You should feel the stretch in the right chest area. Hold this position for two more breaths in and out. Then, roll back to the starting position.
3. Bend your right arm and bring your right hand under your right shoulder to stretch the other side. Breathe

in and exhale as you push into your right hand and roll onto your left hip. Your left arm should be straight and extended. Roll back down to the starting position.

4. Repeat this stretch on both sides two more times.

Take note:

- Roll to the side only as far as it is comfortable for you. As you become more accustomed to the stretch, you will be able to roll farther.

Lower Body Stretches

 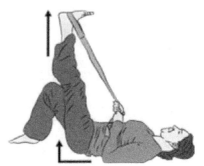

Lying Hamstring Stretch

Areas stretched: hamstrings, glutes.

Instructions:

1. Lie down on the floor with legs straight and arms down by your sides.
2. Raise your left leg, and, with both hands, grab the back of your calf, knee, or thigh to support it. Take a deep breath in, and then exhale. Hold the position for two more breaths and gently bring your leg closer to your body, only if it is comfortable. Finally, lower the leg back to the floor.
3. Stretch the other leg by bringing your right leg up, and with both hands, grab your leg where you can. Breath in deeply and then exhale. Hold the position for two more breaths and attempt to bring your leg closer to your body gently. Lower the leg back to the floor.
4. Repeat the stretch on each side two more times.

Take note:

- Keep your head and upper back on the floor as you raise your leg to avoid straining your neck.
- If you cannot grab your leg with both hands, an alternative is to do this stretch lying next to a wall, bed, or sofa where you can support the lifted leg.

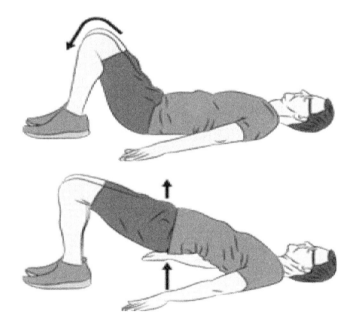

Bridge Pose

Areas stretched: glutes, abdominals, hamstrings.

Instructions:

1. Lie down on the floor on your back with your arms by your sides. Bend your knees so they are pointing up to the ceiling, and bring the back of your heels as close to your glutes as you can.

2. Take a deep breath in and exhale as you push your feet into the floor and lift your hips up and towards the ceiling. There should be a diagonal line from your shoulders to your knees. Hold the position while breathing normally for 30 seconds. It is okay if you can't hold your hips up that long. Lower hips back down to the floor gently.
3. Repeat the stretch four or five more times.

Take note:

*   Don't raise your hips too high. You want to avoid hyperextending your lower back. Your shoulders and hips should be in a line.
*   Maintain good form when doing this stretch. It's better to hold the position for a shorter amount of time but correctly rather than holding it for 30 seconds incorrectly.

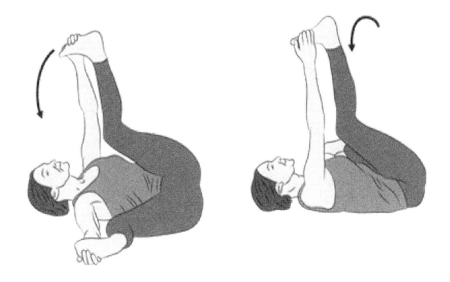

Happy Baby

Areas stretched: inner thighs, hamstrings, groin, lower back, hips.

Instructions:

1. Lie on the floor on your back. Bend your knees and bring them towards you, so your feet are facing up towards the ceiling.
2. Keep your head on the mat as you reach your hands up to grab your feet. You can grab the outer edge or inside arch of your feet, whichever is more comfortable for you. Let your knees fall away from each other, and try to bring your knees to your armpits.
3. Gently rock from side to side, like a happy baby, while keeping your feet flexed. Breathe normally throughout the stretch. You can hold this stretch for several breaths, or whatever is comfortable for you.

Take note:

- Keep your head and shoulders on the floor for the entire stretch. Avoid straining your neck.
- Try grabbing onto your ankles or shins instead if you cannot grab your feet without lifting your head or shoulders.

Square Pose

Areas stretched: hips, inner thighs, spine.

Instructions:

1. Sit on the floor. Bend your left leg on the floor in front of you so that your knee faces towards the left. Next, bend your right leg and put your right shin on top of your left. You should be sitting cross-legged with your right leg directly on top of your left, shins stacked. Breathe in deep, and then exhale. Hold this position for two or three more breaths.
2. To stretch the other hip, change the cross of your

legs with your left leg on top this time. The left shin should be stacked directly on top of the right one. Hold this position for two or three more breaths.

Take note:

- If it is hard for you to sit upright in this position, place a blanket or towel under your tailbone for support.
- To deepen this stretch, fold your upper body forward using your hands on the floor for support. You can either keep your spine straight and long or round your back for a more passive pose.

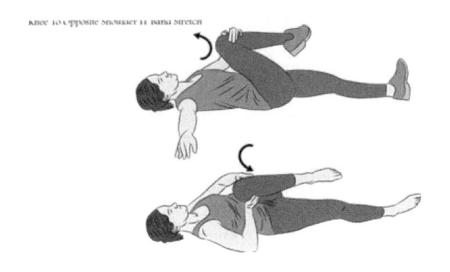

Knee to Opposite Shoulder IT Band Stretch

Knee to Opposite Shoulder IT Band Stretch

Areas stretched: iliotibial (IT) band.

Instructions:

1. Lie on your back on the floor with your legs straight and arms by your sides.
2. Bend and raise your left knee towards you, grabbing behind your knee with both hands. Gently bring your knee towards the right shoulder. You should feel the stretch on the outside of your left hip and thigh where the IT band runs. Take a deep breath in and out. Hold the position for two or three more breaths. Gently lower the leg back to the starting position.
3. To stretch the other leg, raise and bend your right leg. Grab behind your knee and gently bring your right knee towards your left shoulder. Breathe deeply in and then exhale. Hold the position for two or three

more breaths. Gently lower the leg and return to the starting position.

4. Repeat the stretch on both legs two more times.

Take note:

- A tight IT band can cause pain at the knee and hip joints, so go slowly and carefully when doing this stretch. Don't jerk on your knee at any time.
- Keep your head and shoulders on the floor to avoid any neck strain.

Chapter 9

Tools for Stretching

If you think it would be difficult to remain limber at an older age, then make sure to use these devices, resources, and features to help you achieve your stability goals. Be sure to use the most appropriate resources for you personally when it comes to stretching training, as not every single resource is best for every person.

Foam Roller

A foam roller is one of the best devices you can purchase and will help you with your stretch training. It can be painful, too, mainly when you use it first. However, this is a great tool to have if you want good results, particularly in your back and calves.

Lacrosse Ball

A lacrosse ball is another useful tool you could consider buying. These provide you with a way to do self-massage in places where you need some extra support, such as the neck or back. A lacrosse ball helps you to place pressure at a certain point where you can have knots of connective tissues. Eliminating these knotted fibers will help you feel better and quickly become more mobile.

Rope

We have mentioned using stretch bands before, which some give in them, but you can also use a simple piece of rope or even a towel to help make isotopic stretches resistant.

Using a couple of ropes or towels of different lengths can help you improve stretch performance.

Classes

You can take many different classes, which can help by being a local community of like-minded people and by getting a trained teacher to show you how to stretch correctly without hurting yourself. Take the time to find a class that's right for you, and don't be afraid to ask if you can take one class to test it out before you commit to more.

Personal Trainer / Physical Therapist

When you have a specific health issue that needs attention, you will need to opt to work one-on-one with a personal trainer or physical therapist who will make sure that the workouts you're doing can actually help you better rather than making it worse. Your doctor can usually recommend a good physical therapist, and many gyms have personal trainers that can help.

Applications

Phone applications are another perfect way to help you stick to your stretch routine.

Some exercise apps will also allow you to build your own exercise plan where you can add stretches and decide how long each of them you want to do, then let them play.

Then when you're ready to stretch, all you need to do is start the workout and follow the directions along with.

Using a combination of these tools helps you to keep track of your stretch training plan and be successful.

Chapter 10

Posture and How It Affects Your Body

Good posture enhances every area of your life. Our culture doesn't support our innate right to natural posture, but with the right techniques, we can regain our ability to sit, stand, work, and play in a posture that sustains us and keeps us pain-free. Here are some of the many mental and physical benefits of natural posture:

Protect Yourself from Injury

When you try to perform a certain movement, but poor posture has made the necessary muscles too tight or too weak, your body compensates by recruiting other muscles—muscles that aren't in the optimal position to do what you're making them do. As a result, you might get injured when, sooner or later, you accidentally force a muscle to do something it's simply not suited for. Efficient posture protects you from these injuries.

Feel and Look Taller

Embody your natural posture, and you'll feel taller. Practice daily, and you'll actually become taller as your spine becomes less crooked and compressed. And when you start to see the positive changes from practicing daily exercises, you'll be inspired to keep it up and see even better results.

Increase Your Confidence

Good posture equals confidence. You're better prepared to take on each day when you carry yourself with ease and without pain. Altering your body language and posture subconsciously influences your thinking and decision-making. Get ready for friends and family to notice your new and improved attitude.

Get Stronger

Tension is the enemy of the movement. An unbalanced body uses tension instead of strength and flexibility to hold you upright. When your body is aligned, you can move freely, using the correct muscles for each movement instead of recruiting the wrong ones to compensate for weakness. That means any strength training you do will be more effective—and far less likely to cause injuries.

Improve Your Balance

Your sense of balance depends in large part on information that the nerves throughout your body send to your brain via your spinal cord. Good posture keeps your spine long and naturally curved, so those messages can travel freely up and down your spinal cord. Plus, it's mechanically easier for your body to stay balanced when it's properly aligned, instead of having a hip jutting out here or a shoulder hunched forward there.

Sleep Better

It's easier to fall asleep and stay asleep when you don't have pain or muscle tightness keeping you awake. The general feeling of relaxation you get from going about your life with natural posture also makes a difference. Sleeping in a well-aligned position will help you wake up feeling rested and full of energy.

Live Without Back Pain

You get good at what you practice, and posture is no exception. Working on good posture will strengthen the muscles and ligaments along your spine to easily maintain its natural curves. The more you practice, the better you'll get at it until you're completely rid of the slouching and poor posture that once made those muscles and ligaments weak and caused you back pain.

Improve Your Athletic Performance

To perform your best at athletic endeavors, you need to be balanced, supported, and focused. Good posture can make that happen. With your lungs working at full capacity and your circulation at its most efficient, you'll benefit from increased stamina. You'll also be able to kick a soccer ball or swing a tennis racket with better form, making you less likely to injure yourself and more likely to perform well.

Chapter 11

Daily Tips for Staying Flexible

Work on Your Quality of Life

We should discuss your personal satisfaction briefly. Most 60+ers would rather not become a weight to people around them. They likewise don't have any desire to spend each waking moment stuck to the couch since everything simply appears to be a mind-boggling physical exertion.

Tragically, you will be a weight or conceivably stable on the off chance that you don't invest energy staying in shape and dynamic. Your energy and wellness levels won't normally improve as you progress in years. They will absolutely deteriorate. Be that as it may, you can intrude on the descending twisting of going downhill and fixed by stepping in with some solid stretching. Stretching is certifiably not a handy solution; however, it is the key to an existence of 60+ where you can twist and stretch for things effectively, convey your own food, and bear less of a throbbing painfulness route.

We talk from our very own experience when we let you know that stretching makes you more steady, more ready—to do many things—and defter. Just a couple of years before, we didn't play the games we love or go running on Sunday mornings. The risk of injury accompanied regular exercises, and we dreaded the twinges, agonies, and sprains after an energetic morning with the grandkids. All that has changed for us, and it all started with a basic day-by-day stretching program to be very legitimate.

We've, as of now, covered the advantages of beginning your day with a couple of stretches, yet it's a subject definitely worth returning to.

The Benefits of Starting Your Day With Basic Stretches

1. Stretching launches blood dissemination, which initiates the body and psyche with a new surge of supplements and oxygen. Simultaneously, muscles that have been very still for a long time are gradually slipping into activity. The increase in oxygenated blood will likewise provide you with a nice explosion of energy for the afternoon.
2. Stretching strengthens muscles and further develops adaptability, which works on your stance, loosens up muscles, and warms them up.
3. Stretching offers back torment its walking orders! Stretching facilitates strain in the neck and back, as-

sisting with lightning torment while strengthening the muscles simultaneously.

A couple of years ago, we probably wouldn't have accepted that our 60+ lives could change so much. Who would have realized that accomplishing something as basic as stretching could change everything we expected in old age. What's more, since we started getting familiar with the idea of stretching with more than 60+ people around us, we've seen critical improvements in their lives as well. The proof is in putting it all into action. You don't need to put in hours consistently. Instead, you can focus on devoting just 20 minutes a day, four to five days a week. Keep this awake for 21 days, and then conclude what you think and feel. We're willing to bet you won't be able to help but stretch and revel in the physical benefits. When we got everything rolling, we focused exclusively on completing a couple of stretches each day and then consistently before bed. After half a month, we both began to see our energy levels unquestionably amped up; therefore, we opted to move up a level (or three, for that matter). We started slowly, but now we play sports, go for a run, keep an eye on the grandkids, and have a newfound dynamism!

Chapter 12

How to Adapt Stretching Workouts to Physical Limitations

When creating your customized stretching workout, keep the following tips and principles in mind.

Ideally, Hold Static Stretches for 60 Seconds

Based on the current guidelines, you get the most benefit from each static stretch when you hold it for 60 seconds. You can do this by breaking up the stretch, repeating it, say, 2 times for 30 seconds each or 4 times for 15 seconds each. If you want to vary your routine, one easy way to do that is to hold the stretches in the sequences for a total of 60 seconds each.

Sequence Your Dynamic Stretches

When developing your workout of dynamic stretches, start with movements that go from front to back before moving to side-to-side movements. Follow these with rotational movements.

Choose A Variation That Serves You Best Today

Remember, your body is different every day, so when you're putting together a stretching routine, choose variations of the stretches that allow you to perform the movements without pain.

Understand Which Areas You Are Trying to Work on

To make the most of your stretching workout, have a clear understanding of which areas of your body you are targeting with each stretch. Remember that some stretches work multiple parts of your body, offering you more bang for your buck when designing your routine.

Explore Different Stretching Techniques

Although the routines in this book primarily focus on static and dynamic stretching, when creating your own workout, try other forms of stretching, such as Active Isolated Stretching (AIS) and proprioceptive neuromuscular facilitation, which both offer a host of benefits.

Working With a Professional

If you'd rather not go it alone on your stretching journey, enlist the professional guidance of a certified personal trainer who can create a customized stretching workout just for you, taking into account your unique fitness goals as well as other special considerations, such as any existing health conditions you might have. A knowledgeable personal trainer can also teach you the proper form for each stretch, ensuring you get the most benefit from your workouts. Also, a personal trainer can be fun and motivating, holding you to a regular flexibility-training routine, so you continue to make progress toward your goals.

Keep in mind, that just like any profession; not all personal trainers are created equal. To find a professional who has earned a nationally accredited personal training certification, search the United States Registry of Exercise Professionals (USREPS): USreps.org.

Chapter 13

Stretching For Hobbies/Sports

Recreational Pursuits

This series is designed to prevent possible injuries, rehabilitate existing injuries, and balance out the negative results of one-sided activities, such as golf and tennis. For more specific information on sports conditioning, check out Total Sports Conditioning for Athletes 50+ (Ulysses Press, 2008).

Biking/Cycling

Most people would assume that biking is a lower-body activity but think of your posture as you're on the bike. Your body is rounded over the handlebars, with much of your weight resting on your wrists and hands. Start out with an easy warm-up ride. If you're very inflexible, get off the bike and stretch. Otherwise, stretch after your ride and ice sore joints if necessary. If you can, have your bike professionally adjusted to fit you.

Stretches For Biking/Cycling

- Single Knee to Chest
- Standing Quad Stretch
- Double Knee to Chest
- Kneeling Hip Flexor
- Piriformis Stretch
- Rear Calf Stretch
- Gas Pedal
- I, Y, & T
- Torso Relax
- Hamstring/Hip Release
- Ankle Circle,
- Quad Massage
- Foot Massage

Bowling

Many people don't think bowling is a sport, yet it can be very hard on the hips, knees, shoulders, and back. One problem that bowling presents is that it is one-sided, and you are asked to throw a heavy ball with full force. All this can lead to injuries. Practice with a few easy rolls before going full strength.

Stretches for Bowling

- Sit & Reach
- Standing Hip Flexor
- Gas Pedal
- Heel Raise/Heel Drop
- Seated Wrist Stretch

- Inward/Outward Wrist Stretch
- Finger Tap
- Finger Spreader
- Shoulder Box
- Head Tilt
- Tennis Watcher
- Side Bend
- Seated Knee to Chest
- Twister
- Windmill on Roller
- Drop-Off Stretch
- Forearm Massage

Canoeing, Kayaking, or Stand-Up Paddle Boarding

Stand-up paddle boarding (SUP) and paddling sports like canoeing and kayaking are primarily upper body tasks, so pay attention to not getting overly tight through the chest region. Perform a light walk or jog beforehand. If you tend to use only one side to stroke, try to switch sides to balance out your muscle use.

Stretches for Canoeing, Kayaking, Or Stand-Up Paddle Boarding

- Twister
- Tennis Watcher
- Pec Stretch,
- The Zipper
- Picture Frame
- Windmill on Roller

- Neck Massage
- I, Y, & T
- Standing Quad Stretch

Golf

Many people say they play golf, yet I am still waiting to speak to someone who "plays" golf. Most people actually compete in golf and often make an enjoyable pastime a stress-laden event. Golf is tough on the body and hard on the knees, hips, and especially the lower back. One problem with golf is that it is asymmetrical, meaning only one side of the body gets used repeatedly. The other issue is that the worse at golf you are, the harder it is on your body due to more repetition and bad form.

Walk for a few minutes before the match starts; walk the course, if possible. Don't always pull your clubs with the same arm. Similarly, try taking an equal number of swings to the left and right to even out all the one-sided swings you'll be executing in the game. Try to stay as balanced to the left as you are to the right. And, finally, avoid the food and drink at the 19th hole!

Stretches for Golf

- Head Tilt
- Side Bend
- Palm Tree
- Double Knee to Chest
- Rear Calf Stretch
- Standing Wrist Stretch

- Inward/Outward Wrist Stretch
- Finger Spreader
- Shoulder Roll
- Hands behind
- The Zipper
- Elbow Touch
- Windmill on Roller
- Prone Reverse Fly
- Neck Massage

Skiing/Snowboarding

Skiing can be an explosive sport that asks you to per-form hard for short spurts, stand around for a while in line, and then exert full force again. With skiing, you have to contend with the cold at high altitudes, and our 50-plus tendons and ligaments often gel up when left alone in the cold. Skiing is a total-body sport and can be hard on shoulders, knees, and tendons. Always warm up and stop when you are fatigued. Listen to your body. Don't over-ski your ability or fitness level. Ski a couple of bunny slopes before you start the day and finish with a stretch after a warm shower.

Stretches for Skiing:

- Skyscraper
- Palm Tree
- Side Bend
- Sit & Reach
- Standing Quad Stretch

- Standing Hip Flexor
- Rear Calf Stretch
- Ankle Circle
- Seated Wrist Stretch
- Finger Spreader
- Double Wood Chop
- Choker
- Picture Frame
- Over the Top
- Kneeling Hip Flexor
- Inner Thigh Massage
- Hamstring Massage
- Foot Massage

Swimming

Water exercise is gentle on the body and everybody should do it. But swimming is not as kind. Over time, swimming laps can contribute to shoulder problems, and breathing to one side repeatedly can aggravate lower back problems. A few gentle laps to warm-up is always a good idea. Stretch after your laps. It would be wise to have your swim skills analyzed if you swim a lot.

Stretches for Swimming:

- Gas Pedal
- Shoulder Roll
- Double Wood Chop
- Choker
- Over the Top

- Pec Stretch
- Windmill on Roller
- Neck Massage
- Prone Reverse Fly
- I, Y, & T
- Torso Relax

Tennis

Tennis is a fun sport, but it often takes a significant toll on the body. The knees take a pounding and the shoulders are asked to perform some difficult moves. The load placed on the spine, not to mention the cardiovascular system, is tremendous. The fact that it is mostly an asymmetrical game (meaning it is done mostly on one side of the body) sets you up for misalignments.

Stretching is very important if you are a tennis player. Take a few minutes to walk around the court then gently hit the ball back and forth to lubricate the affected joints. Once you're warmed up, take a few moments to stretch before the game starts. Stretch between sets and after the game as well.

Stretches for Tennis

- Double Knee to Chest
- Piriformis Stretch
- Inner Thigh Stretch
- Rear Calf Stretch
- V Stretch
- Ankle Circle

- The Butterfly
- Drop-Off Stretch
- Picture Frame
- Inner Thigh Massage
- Standing Quad Stretch
- Foot Massage
- Pec Stretch
- Rotator Cuff
- Windmill on Roller
- Side Bend with Band
- Kneeling Hip Flexor

Walking/Jogging

Jogging, running, and walking are primarily lower body activities. To incorporate a stretching routine into your regular activities, start out at a slower pace than you usually do. Once you feel warmed up, stop and stretch your hips, legs, knees, and ankles. Don't forget to stretch your chest and shoulders, because often your upper body becomes hunched over. After your exercise, take time to stretch some more.

Stretches for Walking/Jogging:

- Double Knee to Chest
- Standing Hip Flexor
- Rear Calf Stretch
- Gas Pedal
- Ankle Circle
- Windmill on Roller

- Side Bend with Band
- Kneeling Hip Flexor
- Quad Massage
- Hamstring Massage
- Inner Thigh Massage
- Foot Massage

Chapter 14

Powerful Techniques to Make Stretching a Habit

You now have a framework for building stretching as part of your everyday routine, and we hope your dedication won't stop when you put down this book. Scientists estimate it takes anywhere from 18 to 254 days for a person to form a new habit. That may seem like a long time, but it's well worth the investment.

As with forming any new habit, consistency is key. Although 5 or 10 minutes of stretching every day adds up to progress, 5 minutes sporadically won't do much good. To see results, make it a daily practice. However, keep in mind that even the core can be overworked. If you experience a new pain, you may need to take a day of rest. Sore is okay; pain is not!

With long-term, daily use of your routines, you'll begin to feel your muscles becoming stronger. When combined with nutritious food choices and some added aerobic exercise, your clothes will fit a little looser and you'll begin to see more muscle definition. Most important, you'll be lowering your risk factors for disease and decreasing the likelihood of having a fall or other injury.

You needn't rely on willpower alone to form your new habit. These tips will help you be more mindful of making core strength a daily practice.

Make a list of why you're doing it. Whatever your reasons for wanting to improve your core strength, write them down on a piece of paper and tack it up where you can see it. Being reminded of your "why" on a regular basis will help you think of your daily practice as something you *want* to do rather than something you *have* to do.

Set a reminder. If you have a smartphone, it's easy to set a daily reminder. On an iPhone, use the Clock app to set an alarm that goes off at the same time each day, or customize the time for different days of the week. There are also plenty of free apps in the App Store or Google Play Store that you can use to set up calendar notifications, text message reminders, and more. Prefer a more traditional reminder system? Use good old-fashioned sticky notes to remind you to fit in a five-minute session. Sticky notes are also great for short affirmations, such as *"I am strong," "I deserve to be healthy,"* or *"I am in control of my success,"* which will help you maintain a positive mindset.

Make it part of something you enjoy. The best exercise doesn't feel like exercise at all. Make your five-minute sessions more fun by combining them with something you enjoy, such as your favorite Friday night TV show, an upbeat playlist on iTunes, or your phone calls with your grandkids.

Enlist a friend. Use the buddy system and recruit a friend to join your daily core practice, then hold each other accountable. It doesn't have to be someone you see regularly; technology such as FaceTime and Zoom makes it easier than ever to connect with friends and family even if they're on the other side of the country.

With that, we will leave you to get busy building your new, healthy habit. We applaud you for taking the first steps toward a stronger, more mobile, and more pain-free body and we wish you well on the road to self-improvement.

Chapter 15

31-Days Stretching Program

Day 1	Day 2	Day 3	Day 4	Day 5
Overhead Stretch	Neck Roll Stretch	Cat and Cow	Foot Point and Flex	Lying Knees to Chest
Cactus Arms	Seated Spinal Twist	Seated Forward Bend	Half Kneeling Hip Flexor Stretch	All Fours Side Bend
Child's Pose	Door-Assisted Side Bend	Posterior Arm Cradle	Arm Circles	Shoulder Circles
Cat-Cow Stretch	Wall-Assisted Upper-Back Stretch	Arm Stretch Lying Down	Shoulder Hyperextension	Wall-Assisted Bicep Stretch

Day 6	Day 7	Day 8	Day 9	Day 10
Cross Body Shoulder Stretch	Overhead Triceps Stretch	Ear to Shoulder Neck Stretch	Standing Chest Stretch	Standing Torso Twist
Triceps Stretch	Wrist Flexion	Hip Twist	Cobra	Butterfly
Cat-Cow, Bird Dog Sequence	Cat-Cow, Bird Dog Sequence	Cat-Cow, Bird Dog Sequence	Cat-Cow, Bird Dog Sequence	Cat-Cow, Bird Dog Sequence
Wrist Rotation Bicep Stretch	Shoulder Rolls	Eagle Arms Pose	Superman Stretch	Lying Pectoral Stretch

Day 11	Day 12	Day 13	Day 14	Day 15
Bear Hug Seated Overhead Side Stretch Child's Pose Cat-Cow Stretch	Thread the Needle Floor Angels Door-Assisted Side Bend Wall-Assisted Upper-Back Stretch	Child's Pose Banana Stretch Posterior Arm Cradle Arm Stretch Lying Down	Windshield Wipers Stretch Reclined Figure Four Arm Circles Shoulder Hyperextension	Lying Spinal Twist Reclined Butterfly Shoulder Circles Wall-Assisted Bicep Stretch

Day 16	Day 17	Day 18	Day 19	Day 20
Hurdler Hamstring Stretch Seated Overhead Side Stretch Child's Pose Lying Hamstring Stretch	Standing Calf Stretch Floor Angels Door-Assisted Side Bend Bridge Pose	Quad Stretch Banana Stretch Posterior Arm Cradle Happy Baby	Seated Butterfly Reclined Figure Four Arm Circles Square Pose	Standing Lunge Reclined Butterfly Shoulder Circles Knee to Opposite Shoulder IT Band Stretch

Day 21	Day 22	Day 23	Day 24	Day 25
Overhead Stretch Cactus Arms Child's Pose Cat-Cow Stretch	Neck Roll Stretch Seated Spinal Twist Door-Assisted Side Bend Wall-Assisted Upper-Back Stretch	Cat and Cow Seated Forward Bend Posterior Arm Cradle Arm Stretch Lying Down	Foot Point and Flex Half Kneeling Hip Flexor Stretch Arm Circles Shoulder Hyperextension	Lying Knees to Chest All Fours Side Bend Shoulder Circles Wall-Assisted Bicep Stretch

Day 26	Day 27	Day 28	Day 29	Day 30
Cross Body Shoulder Stretch	Overhead Tricep Stretch	Ear to Shoulder Neck Stretch	Standing Chest Stretch	Standing Torso Twist
Tricep Stretch	Wrist Flexion	Hip Twist	Cobra	Butterfly
Cat-Cow, Bird Dog Sequence	Cat-Cow, Bird Dog Sequence	Cat-Cow, Bird Dog Sequence	Cat-Cow, Bird Dog Sequence	Cat-Cow, Bird Dog Sequence
Wrist Rotation Bicep Stretch	Shoulder Rolls	Eagle Arms Pose	Superman Stretch	Lying Pectoral Stretch
Day 31				
Bear Hug				
Seated Overhead Side Stretch				
Child's Pose				
Cat-Cow Stretch				

Conclusion

Stretching has a crucial role in maintaining our body and general well-being as we age. As we have learned throughout this book, stretching is for everyone, not just competitive athletes and professional dancers. Regular stretching can be done anywhere and at any time of the day. Stretching before and after exercise and strenuous activity is a no-brainer, but we saw that stretching in the morning and in the evening is not only beneficial but helps us shift into and out of the events of our day.

There are many wrong ways to stretch that can actually hurt instead of help our bodies, so we learned some things to avoid. Remembering to warm up first before stretching is crucial, as well as being careful not to bounce while stretching. Incorporating a variety of stretches is important to keep our muscles from any imbalances that may occur because of doing the same stretches again and again. The goal is muscle strength as well as symmetry. While we do want to stretch to the point of muscle tension, we have to stop before any stretch becomes painful because this is detrimental to our goal of flexibility and increased range of motion.

One of the aims of this book was to provide a resource for older adults. Having a book that you can turn to again and again as you embark on a journey to better health through stretching is helpful. It is also convenient to have these stretches in one volume. The exercises in each chapter can be mixed and matched according to your personal fitness goal and individual needs. As was mentioned previously, stretching is not a quick fix, but rather a lifestyle choice. Of the factors that contribute to our biological age, or the age at which our bodies function, physical activity is one of the factors that we can easily control and pursue. While our chronological age, or the years we have lived on this planet, can never change, our biological age can. Our body's mobility and flexibility help our biological age to always be younger than our natural years.

All the best to you and to your health!

Excercises Index

Link to a Free Music Playlist for Stretching

https://8tracks.com/swenylo/contortionism

https://8tracks.com/pizzar0lls/stretching

https://8tracks.com/explore/stretching

https://soundcloud.com/atmospheric-music-portal/sets/music-for-yoga-relaxing

https://8tracks.com/naomisl/stretch-work-out

https://8tracks.com/anondancer/stretching-part-1

Glossary

All-Fours Position: Coming down to your hands and knees with your wrists lined up under your shoulders and knees directly below your hips.

Anterior: The front side of the body.

Contraction: Engaging a muscle.

Dynamic Stretching: Quick movements that warm up the body and prepare it for movement.

Flexibility: The ability of each of your joints to move through their full range of motion.

Indication: A factor or reason to perform an exercise.

Passive Stretching: Using an external force to help you go deeper into a stretch.

Proprioceptive Neuromuscular Facilitation (PNF): A technique discovered by physical therapists to contract a muscle while stretching in an effort to get a deeper stretch.

Posterior: The back side of the body.

Resistance Stretching: Passing through a full range of motion in a stretch while applying resistance.

Static Stretching: Staying still and holding a stretch.

References and Research

American College of Sports Medicine ACSM's Guidelines for Exercise Testing and Prescription, 9th ed. Philadelphia: Wolters Kluwer/Lippincott Williams & Wilkins, 2014.

Costa, Pablo B., Barbara S. Graves, Michael Whitehurst, and Patrick L. Jacobs. "The Acute Effects of Different Durations of Static Stretching on Dynamic Balance Performance." Journal of Strength and Conditioning Research 23, no. 1 (January 2009): 141–147. doi:10.1519/JSC.0b013e31818eb052.

González-Ravé, José M., Angela Sánchez-Gómez, and Daniel Juárez Santos-García. "Efficacy of Two Different Stretch Training Programs (Passive vs. Proprioceptive Neuromuscular Facilitation) on Shoulder and Hip Range of Motion in Older People." Journal of Strength and Conditioning Research 26, no. 4 (April 2012): 1045–1051. doi:10.1519/JSC.0b013e31822dd4dd.

Herman, Sonja L., and Derek T. Smith. "Four-Week Dynamic Stretching Warm-Up Intervention Elicits Longer-Term Performance Benefits." Journal of Strength and Conditioning Research 22, no. 4 (July 2008): 1286–1297. doi:10.1519/JSC.0b013e318173da50.

Cho, Sung-Hak and Soo-Han Kim. "Immediate Effect of Stretching and Ultrasound on Hamstring Flexibility and Proprioception." Journal of Physical Therapy Science, vol. 28, no. 6 (June 2016): 1806-1808. DOI: 10.1589/jpts.28.1806

Wong, Alexei and Arturo Figueroa. "Effects of Acute Stretching Exercise and Training on Heart Rate Variability: A Review," Journal of Strength and Conditioning Research (February 2019). DOI: 10.1519/JSC.0000000000003084

Reddy, Ravi Shankar and Khalid A Alahmari. "Effect of Lower Extremity Stretching Exercises on Balance in Geriatric Population." International Journal of Health Sciences, vol. 10, no. 3 (July 2016): 389–395. PMCID: PMC5003582

Edeer, Ayse, Allison Licardo, Alanna Rooney, Danielle Freund, and Valerie Olson. "The Effects of Static Versus Dynamic Stretching on Average Power in The Young-Adult Athletic Population." MOJ Yoga and Physical Therapy, vol. 1, no. 1 (2016): 25–30. DOI: 1.10.15406/mojypt.2016.01.00006

Kim, Giwon, Hyangsun Kim, Woo K Kim, and Junesun Kim. "Effect of Stretching-Based Rehabilitation on Pain, Flexibility and Muscle Strength in Dancers with Hamstring Injury: A Single-Blind, Prospective, Randomized Clinical Trial." The Journal of Sports Medicine and Physical Fitness, vol. 58, no. 9 (October 2017): 1287-1295. DOI: 10.23736/S0022-4707.17.07554-5

Dantas, Estélio H.M., Estevão Scudese, Rodrigo G.S. Vale, Gilmar W. Senna, Ana Paula de A. Albuquerque, Olívia Mafra, Fabiana R. Scartoni, Mario Cezar

S. Conceição. "Flexibility Adaptations in Golf Players During a Whole Season," Journal of Exercise Physiology Online, vol. 21, no. 2 (April 2018): 193–201. https://www.researchgate.net/publication/324074773_Flexibility_Adaptations_in_Golf_Players_during_a_Whole_Season

Printed in Great Britain
by Amazon

24520104R00106